A DETAILED HISTORY OF
RAF MANSTON
1916-1930

A DETAILED HISTORY OF
RAF MANSTON
1916-1930
The Men That Made Manston

JOE BAMFORD AND JOHN WILLIAMS

FONTHILL

Learn more about Fonthill Media. Join our mailing list to
find out about our latest titles and special offers at:
www.fonthillmedia.com

Fonthill Media Limited
www.fonthillmedia.com
office@fonthillmedia.com

First Published 2013

British Library Cataloguing in Publication Data:
A catalogue record for this book is available from the British Library

Typeset in 10pt on 13pt Sabon LT
Printed and bound in England

Connect with us
 facebook.com/fonthillmedia   twitter.com/fonthillmedia

CONTENTS

Foreword

Manston. The very name conjures up visions of epic deeds in Kentish skies during two world wars. When I joined the Royal Air Force as a lowly Aircraftman in 1974, there were still a large number of flying stations on the 'inventory' that could make similar claims to greatness, but somehow the attraction of Manston and its unique setting on the Isle of Thanet seemed more appealing. Small wonder, then, that it appeared at number two on my 'dream sheet' of desired postings as I prepared to graduate from trade training at the Central Air Traffic Control, RAF Shawbury. (The honour of being number one fell to RAF Thorney Island, which held the distinct advantage of being within a short bus ride of my parents' house near Chichester!)

Alas, I quickly came to appreciate the old adage 'If you can't take a joke then you shouldn't have joined' as I found myself posted to RAF Leuchars in Scotland, doubtless yet another victim of the RAF's sense of humour that passed as personnel management in those days. My subsequent career, including commissioning in 1979, took me in different directions, all the time getting further and further away from Manston. Then, out of the blue, in 2004 (but only after a suitable spell spent appreciating England from the vantage point of a hot, dusty Middle Eastern country) I was offered the chance to take up the appointment of Commandant of the MOD Fire Training School. The decision to accept took less than a second. Notwithstanding the endless paperwork, reducing staff and budgetary stresses that are the lot of the modern station commander, I still made time to savour the special atmosphere and history of the unit, which occupies most of the pre-1943 (runway extension) site. I have watched ghost hunters in action, crawled through tunnels and old air-raid shelters, clambered up rickety ladders atop old sheds, and spent hours metal detecting for old artefacts, all in the name of 'CO's inspections' but in reality just exploring a very special place.

Nowhere was this more special than in the nearby Spitfire & Hurricane Museum where the volunteer staff, most of them RAF veterans, proudly kept the RAF flag flying, and many happy hours were spent there swapping stories. Likewise the adjoining RAF History Museum, which has managed to remain delightfully independent and survive to remind us of such exciting times in the past.

At the same time, it is important to acknowledge the work of various authors whose research efforts continue to add to our understanding of the former RAF Manston and in this respect I congratulate Joe Bamford and John Williams on their achievements within this book; there is already space reserved on my groaning bookshelves for the next volume!

Wing Commander David Lainchbury

Acknowledgements

For much of the detailed information in this book I have to thank researcher Peter Gallagher who has tirelessly trawled the records of RAF Manston at the National Archives and found some very valuable material. Peter has been involved with this project for over eighteen months, and without his help and support it is very unlikely that it would ever have materialised.

We have not produced a Bibliography because most of the information has been gathered from official documents such as the Operational Record Books. We have also drawn upon other sources such as *The London Gazette* and *Flight* magazine archive. However, there are two books that we must acknowledge: *The History of RAF Manston* by Rocky Stockman and *Wings Over Westgate* by Geoffrey Williams. Both very credible works in their own right, they have provided the blueprint for the history of RAF Manston that we have followed and expanded into a more detailed account.

Over the years, various people have encouraged us to produce a detailed work on Manston. Among them are Peter Turner, former Curator of the Spitfire & Hurricane Memorial Building; Wing Commander David Lainchbury, the former Commandant of the Fire Training School (FSCTE); and Warrant Officer Derek Crow-Brown, the CMC of the Mess at Manston, who in November 2012 allowed me to give a talk about the history of the station. During the evening I met several people who have been associated with the station, some of whom I had not seen for many years, including David Lainchbury, Peter Turner and Mick Dodsworth. They, like many others who have worked or served at Manston, were most keen that the station's history should be recorded, and provided much encouragement to complete this book.

Thanks also go to Tony Harman of the Kodak shop in Skipton, who has always fulfilled my request for higher resolution images of old photos that have become quite grainy – often at very short notice!

On a final note we must thank Mr Christopher Lofft, the grandson of Flight Sub-Lieutenant Lofft, with whom we made contact just before the final script was handed over to Fonthill Media. Chris has very generously provided many of the valuable photographs and documents that appear in the book. The information they have provided has significantly enhanced not only the visual aspect of the book but the text as well with historical detail that would otherwise have been sadly lacking.

Introduction

We must admit that we found it difficult to know where to begin on a project that details the eighty-three-year history of one of the RAF's oldest and most renowned stations. After much discussion, it was agreed that we should begin with the origins of flight on the Isle of Thanet and around the immediate area of Manston where the airfield was established.

Were it not for the early civilian aviators who regularly visited the island and the Royal Navy's Flying School being established at Eastchurch on the Isle of Sheppey, the Royal Naval Air Station at Westgate would never have been built. Without Westgate, there is little doubt that RAF Manston would never have been established.

During its years of operational service, RAF Manston was the base for numerous units from both the Royal Navy and Royal Air Force that carried out a wide variety of operations, involving every command in the Air Force. In more recent years, in its role as a Master Diversion Airfield, it has been the scene of numerous incidents involving both military and civil aircraft. One of the most dramatic occurred in 1967 when, on 20 April, the British Eagle Britannia G-ANCG made a complete wheels-up landing on a foam carpet and made headlines around the world.

In light of such historic events, and for the sake of simplicity, we decided to proceed in a chronological order. However, in some cases we found it necessary to move the timescale and jump in and out of the years to make it easier for the reader to make sense of things.

It is strange that an airfield with so much history has never been the subject of a detailed publication, although former RAF officers Flight Lieutenant Fraser and Flight Lieutenant 'Rocky' Stockman have produced excellent abridged accounts in their book *The History of RAF Manston*. The first two editions by Flight Lieutenant Fraser (1969 & 1971) were followed up by Rocky Stockman's account in 1986. There was also another book titled *Manston In Old Photographs* produced by the Manston History Club and published by Alan Sutton. All of these works were published before the station finally closed down in 1999, and the purpose of this publication is to give the reader a detailed account of RAF Manston from April 1916.

I was privileged to have served at RAF Manston for two periods – from November 1968 until May 1971, and then again from November 1973 until April 1974. During that time I met a huge number of people, characters who influenced my decision to research and write about the story of the station. One of them was my former shift corporal Peter Turner, who later became the custodian of the Spitfire Memorial Building that opened on 13 June 1981.

Like many other servicemen who were discharged from the RAF at Manston, Peter had decided to stay in the local area. Indeed, the station at Manston has acted like a magnet for many former servicemen, and I also lived in Thanet for eight years after being discharged. Although I later moved north to live in Yorkshire, I still regularly visit the area and try to keep in touch with former friends and colleagues.

Local Thanet historian John Williams has also been instrumental in producing this account, and has been an inspiration in its own right, not only because of his huge collection of photographs but also his personal interest in history and aviation. John worked with Peter Turner for several years in the memorial building as the archivist/historian. Although he served in the Army rather than the Air Force, he has many connections with aviation and has become a font of all knowledge. John's role has now been recognised and he has been made an 'Honorary Blue' and a member of the Mess at Manston.

This book is as much about the officers and men who served at RAF (RNAS) Manston as it is about the units and aircraft that were stationed there. Where possible we have given a brief biography of every Commanding Officer of the station from its opening in 1916. They are certainly proof enough that the determination, character and humility of such officers determined that it was a case of 'The men who made Manston' and not the other way around. With its underground hangars, its own railway station, power station and swimming baths, RAF Manston was indeed a unique place. This first book covers the period from 1916 to 1930.

On a final note, and as Geoffrey Williams has pointed out in his wonderful book *Wings Over Westgate*, it was Winston Churchill who first used the term 'seaplane' during a Parliamentary debate on 17 July 1913. Until then, such machines were commonly termed as waterplanes, floatplanes or hydroplanes. As far as this account is concerned, I have generally used 'seaplane' unless referring to a newspaper article where the machine was specifically described in another way.

CHAPTER 1

Aviation Around Thanet

As in some other parts of the country, the people of Thanet appear to have been aviation minded from an early age, and in March 1910, American aviation pioneer Samuel Franklin Cody visited Ramsgate. On Good Friday that year he gave a lecture at the Royal Palace Theatre, which was then known as the Amphitheatre. This was in the same month that the first Aviator's Certificate was awarded by the Royal Aero Club to Lord Brabazon.

Founded primarily as a club for balloonists in 1901, the Royal Aero Club was integrated into the Fédération Aéronautique Internationale in 1905. Having adopted the 'Royal' title in February 1910, it became the sole organisation to authorise and issue Aviator's Certificates. Although Cody had been credited with making the first flight in Britain on 16 October 1908, he did not receive his certificate (No. 9) until June 1910.

In Ramsgate, Cody explained to his audience that he had taught himself to fly, admitting that was the reason why he had suffered a number of accidents and had been forced to rebuild his aeroplane on several different occasions. He said that he was basically a patent inventor, a daring experimentalist, but definitely not a lecturer. With that said, he began talking about his experiments with man-lifting kites and explained that they were something that had interested him since he was a fourteen-year-old.

A number of photographs of man-lifting kites were projected onto a large screen and it is claimed that the audience were amazed to see that some of them featured the kites carrying passengers, among them Cody's wife and sons, flying high up off the ground with seemingly very little means of support. He explained to the audience that the highest he had ever flown in a kite was 2,660 feet, but he said that during army and navy experiments they had been flown as high as 3,340 feet.

The fact that aviation was a new and dangerous pastime was highlighted on 22 December 1910, when Mr Cecil Grace, pioneer aviator and holder of the Royal Aero Club's Certificate No. 4, went missing. During the morning of the same day,

Grace had already made a successful cross-channel flight from Dover to Calais while competing for the Baron de Forest Prize. Shortly afterwards he embarked upon the return flight to Dover from Calais, but failed to arrive back in England.

The skipper of the Ramsgate smack *San Toy* claimed that at approximately 3.30 p.m. he had seen an aeroplane that had flown at no more than 50 feet over his topmast and then soon afterwards he had heard a loud noise. Some wreckage made up of spars and wires of the type associated with an aeroplane was later spotted in the sea, and a coastguard also reported hearing an aeroplane just off the coast of Ramsgate. Neither Grace nor his Short biplane was ever seen or heard of again.

There are almost no reports or observations about any aviation-related events in east Kent for the year 1911, except for a brief reference to airmen travelling on a charabanc to Dover. There is no mention about who they were or why they were going to Dover, but there are a number of possibilities including the fact that they may have been connected in some way with the Royal Naval Air Station at Eastchurch, as that was one of the few places in Kent where there were airmen in such numbers.

During this period, Britain lagged well behind both France and Germany in air power, and while it was claimed that the former had mustered over 200 aircraft to take part in army manoeuvres, Britain could scrape together no more than a dozen aeroplanes and a couple of airships. Germany was building a powerful fleet of airships that was already three dozen strong and rapidly increasing in number. The growing concern that Britain was falling behind other European powers was a major factor that led to the Royal Flying Corps (RFC) being established on 13 April 1912.

As the Royal Navy already had a flying school at Eastchurch on the Isle of Sheppey, sightings of aeroplanes became more common in the South East. However, many of the machines were flown by civilians, or a small number of elite officers from the Army or Navy who had been among the first airmen to be awarded their Royal Aero Club Certificates.

During the early morning of Saturday 20 April 1912, the air around Ramsgate became filled with an unfamiliar sound and very soon the still relatively unusual spectacle of an aeroplane was observed. Many people had seen planes out at sea or passing high overhead, but on this occasion the craft was a lot lower and it looked as though this one might be going to land. It was first seen flying low over Margate and Broadstairs before circling even lower over Ramsgate, where it descended to make a smooth landing in a cornfield behind St Lawrence College. A huge number of people who had observed the aeroplane from the streets of Broadstairs and Ramsgate rushed to the spot to get their first close-up view of this strange new machine.

It turned out that the pilot of the machine was Lieutenant Spenser Douglas Adair Grey RN, and it was later reported that the aeroplane was a Short

Right: Lieutenant Spenser Grey RNAS, the first airman to land an aeroplane on the Isle of Thanet, 20 April 1912. (*John Williams*)

Below: Spenser Grey's Short S.45 aeroplane in a field adjacent to St Lawrence College. This time-worn grainy image shows the huge crowd that assembled there with a policeman standing with hands on hips looking overwhelmed. (*John Williams*)

S.45 biplane. The type was a derivative of the Short S.36 that had been built specifically for Frank McClean of the Royal Aero Club and it was similarly powered by a 70 hp Gnome engine that gave it a maximum speed of only 60 mph. The aeroplane that Spenser Grey flew was one of two models that had been ordered by the Royal Navy and had been delivered in March. Together with his mechanic, Fred Brown, Grey had taken off from Eastchurch and flown the 55 miles to Ramsgate in just 1 hour and 10 minutes. Whether he realised it or not at the time, Grey was the first airman to land an aeroplane on the Isle of Thanet, and he was credited with that feat.

Lieutenant Spenser Grey, the son of Charles Campbell Grey and Alice Mary Fawconer Galpin, was born in Rio de Janeiro on 10 February 1889. His father had been the Chief Engineer for the Board of Works in Ireland, and there is no doubt that Spenser Grey came from a privileged background and had a good education. He was one of two children in the family; he had an older sister, Dorothy Vernon Grey, who had been born in August 1887.

On 17 August 1911, Spenser Grey had been awarded his Royal Aero Club Certificate (No. 117), having learned to fly on a Farman type aircraft at the Hewlett-Blondeau School based at Brooklands. He had been awarded his 'ticket' after only seven flying lessons and later gained considerable flying experience on aeroplanes that had been built by Blackburn and Short. Before he joined the Royal Navy, Grey had also owned and flown his own aeroplane in the form of a Blackburn Mercury III.

However, the reason that Spenser Grey found himself making a landing near Ramsgate in April 1912 was very simply the fact that his aeroplane was running out of fuel. After landing, he had to rely on the goodwill of the local people and in particular a young boy, who he sent off into the town to get some petrol. In those days it would still have been a rare commodity, and the boy must have known his way around and where to get it. After the boy had returned from his errand, the aeroplane was refuelled before it was pushed back by a group of eager volunteers to the edge of the cornfield close to an isolated cottage. With his aeroplane manually lined up on the field, Lieutenant Grey started the engine, and it is claimed that the bystanders were somewhat surprised by the sudden rush of wind from the propeller wash that blew off their hats and ruffled their hair.

According to eyewitness reports, the aeroplane rumbled across the field for twenty yards before it became airborne and flew off in the direction of Broadstairs. However, Grey turned the aeroplane around to return to the field before flying low over St Lawrence College and climbing away to disappear out of sight. So ended the first visit of an aeroplane to Thanet and the first ever flypast!

Spenser Grey started something of a trend. Within a matter of days it was noted that a number of aeroplanes from the Royal Naval School at

Eastchurch were seen descending over Margate, Ramsgate, and Broadstairs. It was reported in the *East Kent Times* on 24 April that Thanet had seemingly been invaded by airmen from the Naval School of Aviation at Eastchurch and that they found it very convenient as a place for landing. In the same article it was reported that the Admiralty had purchased ten acres of land adjoining the Royal Aero Club's flying ground at Eastchurch for the newly formed School of Flying. There were regular sightings of Royal Navy hydroplanes off the coast of Westgate and Broadstairs, although their presence and activities were still seen as something of a novelty.

Although not directly connected to the Manston story, eighteen months later, on 8 October 1914, Spenser Grey was awarded the Distinguished Service Order after taking part in a daring raid on Zeppelin sheds at Düsseldorf. The two Sopwith Tabloids that took part in the raid had flown from the Belgian airfield of Wilrijk near Antwerp and although Grey actually failed to find the Zeppelin sheds, he bombed Cologne railway station instead. As it happened, the pilot of the other aircraft, who was also to have a direct connection with Manston very soon, did find the sheds at Düsseldorf, which he destroyed along with Zeppelin L9. He was also subsequently awarded the Distinguished Service Order (DSO).

Commander Charles Rumney Samson and Lieutenant Arthur Longmore were two of the first four officers to have passed out from the Royal Navy's Flying School at Eastchurch and were also among the first airmen to land in Thanet. They arrived on 22 April, the Monday following Spenser Grey's visit, with the former descending and landing on the football ground at Hartsdown, Margate. Having breakfasted with Lieutenant Grey, who had returned to Thanet and stayed over for the weekend at the Queen's Highcliffe Hotel, they flew back to Eastchurch together, taking off at eight o'clock.

Lieutenant Longmore was not so fortunate. Because one of the valves of the six-cylinder engine in his Blériot monoplane was not working properly, he had to make something of a forced landing in a wheatfield near Quex Park. Although he was accompanied by a mechanic, he seemingly did not have the knowledge or the equipment to make a repair and so was forced to ring Eastchurch to get some help. Later in the morning a party of mechanics arrived by motorcar, and within a short time they had repaired the faulty engine. Longmore was an aviation pioneer in his own right, and a naval officer destined for high office. He had been brought up in the town of Manly in New South Wales, Australia, but was educated in England at Benges School in Hertford and Foster's Academy in Stubbington.

Most service pilots flew biplanes during this period, and from later in the year, during September 1912, after a spate of serious accidents, the War Office imposed a temporary ban on its personnel flying monoplanes. The mechanics from Eastchurch soon repaired Longmore's engine and he eventually departed

Commander Charles Rumney Samson at Westgate while *en route* from Dover to Sheerness in 1912. The aircraft had suffered an engine failure and was taken in tow by HMS *Hibernia*. (*John Williams*)

Deperdussin Monoplane powered by a 70-hp Gnome engine that had been flown from Paris to Eastchurch in April 1912 by Maurice Prevost. The first RNAS pilot to fly it was Lieutenant A. M. Longmore. In September 1912 it took part in army manoeuvres and in 1913 it was regularly flown by Lieutenant Spenser Grey. This photo was taken at Quex Park on 22 April 1912 after Lieutenant Arthur Longmore had been forced to land after trouble with the engine's valve gear. (*John Williams*)

for Eastchurch at eleven o'clock. By that time, however, word had got out and an enormous crowd had gathered near Quex, coming on foot or by bicycle, but many of them arriving just in time to see the aeroplane disappearing into the distance.

Charles Rumney Samson, from Manchester, was twenty-nine years old and had only recently been promoted to the rank of commander after serving in the Royal Navy since 1897, when he had trained at the Britannia Royal Naval College in Dartmouth. He had a lot of experience of ships and naval aviation, having served on both HMS *Pomone* and HMS *Commonwealth* and commanded Torpedo Boat No. 81. He had also been the Commanding Officer of RNAS Eastchurch and the Royal Naval Flying School that was based there, as well as being involved in various aspects of early aviation. These included the development of a bomb dropping sight and experimental night landings without the use of lights. More recently, in January 1912, he had carried out the first experimental take-offs from a ship at anchor and then a moving ship at sea in the form of HMS *Hibernia*. Landing on the stable football ground at Hartsdown presented few difficulties for an officer who had already carried out such dangerous and innovative actions. Shortly after his visit to Thanet, on 12 May, Samson was promoted to the position of Commandant of the Naval Wing of the RFC.

On 26 April, the arrival of both Spenser Grey and the other two airmen from Eastchurch was reported in the local newspaper with the headline 'Airmen At Margate'. It claimed that the flights had created such a keen interest in aviation that on the following Thursday huge crowds had gathered both at Hartsdown and Dane Park after rumours had spread that more aeroplanes were about to arrive. The paper reassured its readers that although none had turned up on that occasion, the following week they would soon be as plentiful as 'Policemen'. It advised its readers that those who rose with the lark were more likely be rewarded!

Commander Samson arrived in Thanet again on 13 May, although on that occasion his visit had not been planned but became necessary when the 100 hp Gnome engine of his Short Tractor seaplane failed and he had no option other than to make a forced landing near Westgate. He had been flying from Dover to Sheerness and after being taken in tow by HMS *Hibernia* had to complete the final part of his journey in a much more difficult environment on the water.

Grey, among others, became a regular visitor to Thanet, and it was noted that he had flown down to Margate on 30 May 1912. On that occasion he was flying a Short S.45 biplane powered by a 70 hp Gnome engine. One of the first most regularly used flying grounds in the area was near the power station at St Peter's, Broadstairs, and by that time aviation in Thanet was fairly well established and many other improvised fields and pieces of open ground were used.

A close-up low-level view of Salmet's Blériot when he was visiting Herne Bay on 13 August 1912, prior to a flight along the coast to Thanet. (*John Williams*)

One airman who regularly used the landing ground at St Peter's, which at that time formed part of Callis Grange Farm, was the Frenchman Henry Salmet. Flying his 80 hp Blériot monoplane from Eastchurch, he had first landed there on 12 August 1912. Salmet's tour was part of the *Daily Mail's* 'Wake Up England' campaign run by its owner Lord Northcliffe, its main aim being to alert the general public to the potential of military aeronautics. This was as a result of the dismal prophesies made in the novel *The War In The Air* (first published in 1908) by H. G. Wells, who also wrote a column for the *Daily Mail*.

The well-known aviation company run by British aviator Graham White also visited Margate in August as part of a South Coast waterplane tour organised by the *Daily Mail*. The tour was being carried out for the very same reason as that of Henri Salmet. The Farman F.22 that was flown by a Mr Travers and Mr Noel actually had the words 'Wake Up England' stencilled on its side and it gave both exhibition and passenger flights. More importantly, it gave many ordinary people the opportunity to get close to a flying machine for the first time, and to become familiar with its capabilities – in the opinion of some – to bomb people to oblivion. The waterplane remained at Margate for nearly a week between the 16th and 20th, and the Town Council agreed to provide facilities such as security. At night it was housed on the east side of the tower promenade at the Fort Pavilion near the Winter Gardens.

Two views of the Farman F.22 at Margate in August 1912 during the 'Wake Up England' campaign sponsored by Lord Northcliffe. The aeroplane was flown by a Mr Noel & Mr Travers. (*John Williams*)

M. MANIO AND COASTGUARD OFFICIALS AT MARGATE
BEFORE PARTING WITH HIS DOG 'JIM' WHICH
LEFT FOR

Italian aviator Count Jean Bapisto de Manio at Margate on 2 December 1912, after flying from Boulogne accompanied by Coastguard officials and holding his dog 'Jim'. Shortly after this photo was taken the dog was put into quarantine. (*John Williams*)

Another European aviator, Italian-born Count Jean Batista de Manio, a colonel in the Italian Army, was also a regular visitor to Thanet, and on Sunday 12 December he landed his Blériot monoplane near the Admiralty Signalling Station at Kingsgate after flying across the Channel from Boulogne. His only passenger was his dog, Jim, with which he posed for a photo, along with a policeman and a number of naval ratings. An interesting thing to note about Count de Manio is that he was the father of the well-known BBC broadcaster Jack de Manio (Giovanni Batista de Manio) who was born in 1914 and died in 1988. Unfortunately, Jack never knew his father because he had been killed in a flying accident some time before he was born.

On 19 February 1913, the *East Kent Times* ran a story about 'Britain's Peril in the Air', claiming that the British Isles were at the mercy of German airships, and there was a great deal of fear that the Kent coast could come under attack, if not be invaded. Being so close to the Continent, it is hardly surprising that there were restrictions in place to control where aeroplanes could fly, and there were a number of prohibited areas. Dover, just seventeen miles down the road from Ramsgate, was one of them.

Less than a hundred years earlier, the English Channel had been the scene of a number of bitter battles between French and English forces. Although the feared French invasion never happened, there are a number of graves in a small cemetery behind Dover Castle, not far from the Blériot Memorial, of some English soldiers who were killed in skirmishes with the French near the castle during the early part of the nineteenth century. The headstones on the graves (now removed) are proof enough that although the French never actually invaded, they did land on English soil on what were probably small-scale raids.

Fortunately for Thanet and the future RNAS station at Manston, the Home Office declared the airspace between Margate and Walmer to be a non-prohibited area. That decision was almost certainly instrumental in attracting visiting aviators to Thanet, and it became the scene of a number of events such as the first Circuit of Britain Seaplane Race that began at Southampton, with Ramsgate Harbour being chosen as the first checkpoint.

The air race took place on Saturday 16 August 1913, and one of the favourites to win was the famous Australian pilot Harry George Hawker, who was flying a Sopwith Seaplane. Samuel Franklin Cody was one of the other contestants who had entered the race, but he was killed just a few days before the race while flying his Cody Waterplane on Laffan's Plain near Aldershot. Cody's plane was flying at about 500 feet when it broke up in the air and both Cody and his passenger, cricketer William Evans, were killed instantly.

To commemorate Colonel Cody, the King's Theatre in Ramsgate showed a film of his funeral held at the Aldershot Military Cemetery and it was screened at each performance of every other film for a week. French aviator Henri Salmet was one of several people who helped to raise money for the Cody Memorial Fund by selling his autograph while on a tour of the north of England. From that alone he raised £25, which was donated to the Aerial League, while Mrs Cody eventually received £1,325. Probably as a mark of respect the small number of other entrants in the Circuit of Britain Race withdrew, leaving just Harry Hawker in his Sopwith Seaplane.

It is important to note that at this time there were no safety regulations or registration system for aeroplanes – and they would not be introduced for another six years. Aviation was in its infancy and there were no laws regulating the behaviour of airmen or the maintenance of their machines. Technically, civil aviation was outside the law because no legislation had yet been passed that allowed airmen to build and fly their own machines, and there were very few restrictions placed upon pioneering aviators.

On the morning of the race, Harry Hawker, with his passenger, fellow pilot and engineer, Harry Kauper, descended towards Ramsgate Harbour in the Sopwith Seaplane just after 8 a.m. and gently landed on the water of the outer harbour at 8.10. Weather conditions were ideal, with just a light

Sopwith Tractor Seaplane (described as a 'Hydroplane') in Ramsgate Harbour. It was taking part in the 'Around Britain Seaplane Contest' in 1913. It was flown by Australian airman Harry Hawker, who was accompanied by engineer Harry Kauper and it carried the Race Number '1'. (*John Williams*)

breeze and the sun sparkling on the water, encouraging huge crowds to form quickly on both piers. The aeroplane displayed the race number '1' on its tail that was rather appropriate as it was the only aeroplane in the 'Race'. It was immediately surrounded by a flotilla of small boats, one of which carried the two members of the Royal Aero Club who had been appointed to oversee the aeroplane's arrival.

Hawker and Kauper were two of what were referred to as the 'Three Harrys', Harry (Henry) Busteed being the third. They were all from Australia, but had travelled to Britain to study aviation and learn to fly. By 1912, Kauper was employed by Sunbeam as a mechanic/engineer, but later became the Works Manager for Sopwith in charge of 3,800 workers and a company that produced forty-five aeroplanes a week. He was also involved with Sopwith in developing what became known as the Sopwith-Kauper interrupter gear. First tested in April 1916, the mechanism that allowed aeroplanes to fire their guns through the propeller was widely adopted, and 3,950 were fitted to various types. Busteed was the second Australian who had learned to fly, and was awarded his Royal Aero Club Certificate (No. 94) on 13 June 1911.

On the same day as the Circuit of Britain Race was taking place, Sydney Pickles flew low over Margate while *en route* from Folkestone to the Isle of Grain, and a few years later he would become another well-known aviator in the area. Also on the same day as the race, renowned Frenchman Henri Salmet arrived in Thanet again, almost exactly a year since his first tour. He was taking part in another of the *Daily Mail*'s 'Wake Up England' campaigns, and he flew over Ramsgate Harbour just after Hawker had landed. The second time around, however, the newspaper's campaign was not as well received, and it might have been that the Australian had stolen the Frenchman's 'limelight'. Salmet was later engaged in giving pleasure flights from a piece of land loaned by the council in Cliftonville, and it was reported that he took a total of nine people up in two hours.

After having his aeroplane serviced and refuelled in Ramsgate, Harry Hawker took off for the next stage of the race to Yarmouth at 3 p.m. When he arrived there he was quite ill because exhaust fumes had leaked into the cockpit and he had little or no choice but to breathe in the noxious gases. As a result, he was unable to continue with the race and the Royal Aero Club ordered a fresh start to be made, with Hawker arriving back in Ramsgate on Monday 25 August. Even the second time around he aroused a great deal of public interest, and there were large crowds to welcome him.

Henri Salmet with his Blériot Monoplane near the Melrose Hotel in Cliftonville, 'drumming up' custom for his pleasure flights in August 1913. In two hours he took up nine passengers. (*John Williams*)

Above: Salmet's Blériot landing at Cliftonville. (*John Williams*)

Left: Another close-up of Salmet's Blériot during the 'Daily Mail 1913 Tour'. The word 'Mail' is just visible underneath the port wing and a young man in the background is wearing a sweater with the 'Daily Mail' printed on it. (*John Williams*)

A Short's 'Gun Carrying' Seaplane S.81 powered by a 160-hp engine in Ramsgate Harbour during August 1914, after it landed there in bad weather. It was initially fitted with a Vickers 1½-lb fast firing gun but that was later changed to a 6-lb Davis gun for trial on the Isle of Grain. It was scrapped in October 1915. (*John Williams*)

Hawker took off from Ramsgate Harbour again at 9.05 a.m. and by the following day he had reached Oban in Scotland, a distance of 836 miles from Southampton. But disaster struck on the next leg, just before reaching Dublin. Fellow pilot and mechanic Harry Kauper broke his arm in an accident and that proved to be the end for both men. Regardless of the fact that they had been forced to pull out of the *Daily Mail*'s competiton, Hawker was awarded the prize of £1,000, but it was not until some months later that he returned to Ramsgate to be presented with a silver cup by the Mayor of the Ramsgate.

The story of Hawker's seaplane is typical of the period when the RNAS had to rely on private owners and operators to provide aeroplanes that might be of some use to the services. In October 1913, Hawker's Short Seaplane was converted to a landplane, but was involved in a number of crashes. It was later acquired by the Naval Wing and after undergoing testing during April 1914 it was officially accepted on 12 May. However, in July, when the Sopwith machine was demonstrated at the Review of the Fleet, it was recognised that it would not be suitable for naval observation work and the machine was eventually scrapped in August 1914. Hawker went on to become Chief Test Pilot for the Sopwith Aviation Company.

Quex Park with its large open grounds became a popular location for aviators to land and certainly, as had been noted in the local newspapers, by 1913, aeroplanes were beginning to be regarded in Thanet with as little curiosity as a pleasure steamer. On 11 November 1913, no fewer than three aeroplanes landed in the grounds near Quex Park: Lieutenant Conran in a monoplane, accompanied by Lieutenants Chumley and Stockford, who were flying biplanes.

Count de Manio was in the news again in December 1913, when on several occasions he managed to get himself lost. On Wednesday 5 December, on a flight from Sittingbourne to Hendon, he ended up flying over the Bank of England and failed to find the aerodrome. The following Sunday he took off from the sands near Boulogne and was intending to fly to Folkestone, but strong south-westerly winds blew him off course. He struggled through mist and rain and eventually reached Margate, having succeeded in making the first ever crossing of the English Channel in winter.

What was to happen in the following years was no surprise to many when Thanet got its own air station – one that would eventually rival that across the water at Eastchurch. By the end of 1913, the man who had started it all off, Lieutenant Spenser Grey, had been promoted and given command of the Royal Naval Air Station at Calshot.

CHAPTER 2

RNAS Westgate

With so many airmen showing an interest in the East Kent coast, it seemed almost a natural development when the Royal Naval Air Service (RNAS) chose St Mildred's Bay as the location of a base for its seaplanes. It was one of a number of RNAS stations situated in the area, including the very first one to open at Eastchurch on the Isle of Sheppey, which was effectively the birthplace of the RNAS.

The RNAS originated in November 1910, when Frank McClean, a founding member of the Royal Aero Club and landowner on the Isle of Sheppey, offered two Short aeroplanes on which the Royal Navy could train its pilots, plus the use of the instructors and facilities of the aero club. McClean was the founding father of the Royal Aero Club and held its Certificate No. 21.

In early December, the Commander-in-Chief of Nore Command accepted his offer and set up a scheme to train its first pilots, but it was stipulated that candidates had to be single and should be able to afford the membership fees of the Royal Aero Club. There were over 200 applicants, but only four successful candidates were chosen to fly and train to gain their Royal Aero Club Certificate: Lieutenants Charles Rumney Samson (Certificate No. 71 dated 25 April 1911); Arthur Murray Longmore (Certificate No. 72 dated 25 April 1911); Reginald Gregory (Certificate No. 75 dated 2 May 1911); and Captain Eugene Louis Gerrard (Certificate No. 76 dated 2 May 1911). Lieutenant Longmore became the first Australian to be awarded a Royal Aero Club Certificate.

The original flying field at Leysdown was shared with the Royal Aero Club, but McClean gave the Navy another piece of land in 1911 on which to form an air station, which became the home of the Royal Naval Flying School, Eastchurch. A number of small airfields situated on the Isle of Sheppey were used by the Royal Aero Club from 1909, but Eastchurch can claim to be the birthplace of British aviation. Muswell Manor, often referred to as Leysdown, was the original landing ground, but when it proved unsuitable, the adjacent land at Eastchurch was used and it soon became an RNAS station in its own right during 1911. Leysdown then became a relief landing ground for Eastchurch.

Another ten officers of the Royal Navy graduated from the RFC's Central Flying School at Upavon in Wiltshire in April 1913. By June 1914, a total of 44 officers and 105 men had been trained either at the Central Flying School or with the RNAS at Eastchurch. In July 1913, the RNAS was officially formed out of the Military Wing of the RFC.

In November 1913, the Royal Aero Club amended the strict rules that had to be followed by those aviators who wanted to qualify for its certificate. Among them were that an aviator had to fly a distance of at least five kilometres (3 miles 185 yards) in a closed circuit without touching the ground or water. The course was to be marked out by two posts or buoys that were to be at least 500 metres (547 yards apart), and aviators were to fly alone and their actions witnessed by an observer at all times. It all sounds very easy, but it has to be remembered that aeroplanes were primitive machines and aviation was then a very dangerous business.

There were eventually two RNAS air stations on the Isle of Grain, but so as not to be confused with the original site, the second one was named Port Victoria after the local railway station. Port Victoria was, however, not a normal station but one that involved research and experimentation. A number of Sopwith floatplanes were adapted and rebuilt there, and were even given their own prefix 'P.V.' Aeroplane types numbered P.V.1 to P.V.9 were manufactured there, as well as a reconnaissance aircraft called the Grain Griffon, which was a development of the Sopwith B.1.

Because the RNAS stations were situated just across the Swale Channel and close to Thanet, aerial activity was regularly if not commonly seen to be taking place. It was not unusual for aeroplanes to be observed out at sea, and Ramsgate Harbour was one of a number of places along the coast that became a popular place to take refuge in bad weather or when things went wrong.

On 2 August 1912, seaplane No. 126 force landed on the sea near the outer harbour after it had been damaged by strong winds. The machine was later dismantled and taken by motor traction engine to Sheerness. On another occasion, a Lieutenant Bradshaw came ashore from Ramsgate sands after the propeller of his aeroplane had been damaged. He, together with his passenger mechanic, had flown all the way from the Solent.

The first recorded movement of a seaplane at Westgate occurred on 15 June 1914, when three aeroplanes were sent there from the Isle of Grain, for a three day visit, to observe a fleet firing exercise that was being held off the east Kent coast. As might be expected, their arrival was mentioned in the local papers, and the *East Kent Times* in its edition of 17 June named Captain P. Owen as the Officer Commanding the flight, together with fellow

A Fairey Seaplane being pushed into the sea at the Royal Naval Air Station Westgate on Sea. (*John Williams*)

pilots Lieutenant F. G. Brodribb and Lieutenant F. E. T Hewlett. By late 1914, Brodribb, Babington and Longmore were stationed at Calshot and appear together in a group photo of the unit's personnel. Before that, however, Lieutenant J. T. Babington had become strongly associated with the local Westgate area.

The land around the seaplane base at Westgate was not requisitioned until 28 July 1914, and Flight Commander John Tremayne Babington was the station's first Commanding Officer. He arrived at Westgate a few days later on 2 August, flying in a seaplane, No. 120, having been posted in from No. 1 Squadron RNAS. Since visiting Westgate the previous month, Babington had been promoted from the rank of lieutenant.

Commissioned into the Royal Navy in 1908 as a Midshipman and having been awarded the Royal Aero Club Certificate in January 1915, Babington was later to become one of the most decorated and distinguished officers in the service. Just two days after he took up his post at RNAS Westgate, Britain declared war on Germany and the need to organise things more effectively became much more urgent. The strength of the RNAS was just 93 aeroplanes, six airships, two balloons, and 720 personnel.

Two hangars were built at Westgate, the larger being 180 feet long and 60 feet wide, and the smaller one 70 feet long and 70 feet wide. The task of moving the seaplanes from the hangar to the water fell to a group of airmen called 'seaplane waders', but it is not known if that was an official title. It has been claimed that this work was carried out by naval ratings who had not yet gained their trade qualifications and others who had failed their examinations. No doubt on a bad day everyone would have got involved with this heavy work including, very occasionally, the air crew.

Because of the outbreak of war there was an urgent need for naval personnel elsewhere, and as Westgate was the most recent station to open, it was effectively the first to be closed down and put on Care and Maintenance (C&M). The few staff left behind were under the command of Lieutenant Bertie Ingham, the son of local businessman Sir William Ingham, the owner of St Mildred's Hotel and many other establishments in Westgate. Bertie had only recently joined the Royal Naval Air Service Reserve, and it is quite likely that nepotism was instrumental in him being selected.

The war had no immediate impact in the Thanet area, but the local Territorials were mobilised at 7 p.m. on 4 August, as were the Territorial units of 'The Buffs' on the 7th, who marched out of the town and were later sent to India. The first wounded Belgian soldiers began to arrive in October and the Sailors' Rest Home in Ramsgate was used as a temporary hospital. The most alarming incident in the area, although not actually in Thanet, was the sinking of the Royal Navy gunboat HMS *Niger* while it was at anchor off the coast of Deal. It was sunk by a torpedo fired from the U-boat U.12 on 12 November, but the crew were taken off by the Deal and Kingsdown lifeboats just a short while before it exploded. The whole scene was played out in front of a huge crowd of onlookers who had gathered on the shore to witness the remarkable incident.

The German Air Service had established seaplane bases at both Zeebrugge (Flanders 1) and Ostend, and the activity of its crews put both shipping and RNAS aeroplanes in danger of being attacked. On 24 December 1914, a single 22 lb bomb was dropped on Dover by a German Friedrichshafen FF.29 floatplane of Flieger Abteilung 1, and despite the fact that nobody was injured, the incident created panic among the local population. The attack followed an aborted assault on Dover Harbour three days before by seaplanes from the same unit. The two-seat FF.29, powered by a single Mercedes engine, had been introduced into service by the German Navy only in November and the type was used mainly for reconnaissance work.

As a result of the raid on Dover, the RNAS seaplane base at Westgate was reactivated immediately, with a standing order for two seaplanes to be on standby in case enemy aeroplanes or airships approached the Thames Estuary. Patrols were also to be flown from Westgate and other RNAS bases along the coast to provide complete cover against enemy raiders.

Thanet experienced its first air raid on 17 May 1915, when approximately twenty-five bombs fell on the town, and the Bull & George public house in the High Street, where two people were killed, was among a number of buildings that were badly damaged. Most of the bombs were of the incendiary type, and a number of other people were injured when other parts of the town, such as Albion Place, were hit. On 31 May, a Zeppelin was observed passing over the St Lawrence district of Ramsgate, and another one was spotted near Broadstairs on 6 June at 11.40 p.m. Rumours that the Germans were using gas bombs created panic, with a huge number of people buying respirators.

At some unknown point, the Isle of Thanet Emergency Committee published a leaflet headed 'Notice to the Civil Population in case of Emergency', which was specifically produced for the Parish of Manston. It stated that should it be necessary for members of the civil population to be removed, they were strictly to follow its instructions. Those who wished to leave the area were told to proceed via Pouce's, to Way Hill, then Lower Hill Road, Minster, Monkton Road and Pluck's Gutter Bridge to Canterbury. Where possible, transport would be provided to collect the aged, infirmed, young children and their carers, but all others were told that they must travel by foot.

It was ordered that all children under five were to be labelled, and that people were to take all necessary clothing, boots and blankets to protect themselves from the weather as well as all available money and food. Such an exodus was to be controlled by the police and the special constabulary, and it was emphasised that their instructions were to be strictly followed. The notice was signed by Mr. P. H. G. Powell-Cotton, who was Chairman of the Emergency Committee. Whether this scheme was put into practice or if any individuals decided to take up this offer is not known, but it clearly shows that the authorities were prepared to evacuate the area if necessary.

One problem with seaplanes was the amount of time that it could take them to get airborne: a single aeroplane might take five minutes or more to get into the air. When faced with imminent attacks from incoming enemy machines the time factor was important, and with rough sea conditions it could take a lot longer. There were times when a heavy swell could mean that they might not get airborne at all. A number of pilots at Westgate had the experience of not being unable to 'unstick' their seaplane, even on the calmest water. By comparison, it normally took just a couple of minutes for a land-based aeroplane to take off, and that might have been one of the reasons why the RNAS decided to use landplanes at Westgate.

It was not until January 1915 that the RFC flew its first night-time air defence patrol in Britain because of its much needed commitment to fly patrols on the Western Front in France. Up to that point, Home Defence had been almost totally the responsibility of the RNAS, but the increase in activity of the Zeppelin airships meant that the RFC had to supply aeroplanes for Home Defence and provide standing patrols. The first seaplanes to be permanently based at Westgate arrived in February 1915. They were a detachment of 'A' Flight from No. 2 Squadron RNAS that had been formed at Eastchurch the previous October.

The patrols flown by the seaplanes based at Westgate were mainly to monitor shipping, and a number of light vessels were positioned in the North Sea to guide them. The light vessels were also able to listen out for and give warnings of any airships that were approaching the English coast. Up the road from Westgate was the North Foreland Lighthouse, and just off the coast were the North Goodwin and South Goodwin light vessels. Further to the east were the East Goodwin light ship and the Sandettie light vessel; to the north of the North Foreland were the Tongue, Princess Channel and Edinburgh light vessels; and to the north-east of the Edinburgh was the Kentish Knock that was close enough to both the English and Belgian coasts where aeroplanes and seaplanes of both sides challenged each other for superiority of the air and sea.

In the Medway Estuary just to the north of Sheerness was the Nore light vessel. This marked a sandbank that had given its name to the Royal Navy's Nore Command, which controlled the RNAS station at Westgate and several others along the south-east coast. The Nore Command had first been established in 1752, and the Commander-in-Chief of the Nore was effectively the Operational Commander of the Royal Navy. From 1911 until 1915, that position was held by Sir Richard Poore until he handed over the command in 1915, when Sir George Callaghan took up the appointment.

In January 1915, the land on the cliff-top to the east of the seaplane base at Westgate was requisitioned for the use of the RNAS landplanes, but that was the beginning of troubled times at the station. The main problem was that a number of both pilots and senior officers were of the opinion that the landing ground was not long enough for them to get airborne or land safely, especially when they were operating at night. Ironically the site had been considered to be the best of the three examined by Wing Captain Scarlett who had been accompanied on his inspection of Westgate by Lieutenant Herbert Ingram.

It is claimed that it was local man Ingram who pointed out to Scarlett the advantages of the Westgate site, in that it already had wireless telegraphy and telephone facilities connected and a workshop that was used by the seaplane base. The land was subsequently requisitioned from Bethlem Hospital, but despite its size – being half a mile long and a quarter of a mile wide – it was to prove a dangerous piece of ground because of its location on the cliff-top.

The first RNAS fatality on the landing ground at Westgate was twenty-three-year-old Flight Sub-Lieutenant Reginald Lord from Felton in Northumberland, who was killed on 9 August 1915, although the circumstances that led to his death may have been attributable to operational conditions rather than being directly connected to the state of the airfield. The son of Albert Alexander and Emma Louise of Highfield Hall, Newcastle upon Tyne, Lord had been educated privately at Mill Hill School in London. Before joining the RNAS, he had worked in banking and at the Burton House Bank from 1905 until 1909. He had been awarded his Royal Aero Club Certificate, No. 915, on 27 September 1914 after only 2 hours and 33 minutes' flying time

Five German Zeppelin airships, including Zeppelin L12, had been detected approaching the English coast near Westgate from a westerly direction, with three of them heading directly for the Thames Estuary. At 10.48 p.m., L12 was reported to be just off the coast of Westgate, and a number of aircraft were sent up to try to intercept it, including Lord, who took off in a Sopwith Tabloid, No. 1212, at 10.51 p.m. He soon, however, fell foul of the atrocious weather conditions, and in thick fog and very bleak conditions attempted a landing on the cliffs at Westgate. When he was heard approaching the flare path, a searchlight was lit to aid his landing. At first his Tabloid appeared to be making a normal approach, but then it suddenly dipped and hit the ground fifty yards short of the first flare The machine turned over twice and was completely wrecked, and although Lord was badly injured, he was still alive when taken to Margate Cottage Hospital but died soon afterwards. He was buried in Margate Cemetery on 12 August. At the time of his death he was engaged to be married to Miss Violet Beevor, the daughter of Lieutenant-Colonel Beevor of the Scots Guards.

The detachment of 'A' Flight's seaplanes from No. 2 Squadron moved out of Westgate in July and was temporarily replaced by a number of seaplanes from the RNAS station at Dover. In September, Westgate's own War Flight, sometimes referred to as the 'Nore Flight', was formed, and with the new establishment came a new commander.

On 20 September 1915, Squadron Commander Robert Peel Ross was appointed as the Commanding Officer of RNAS Westgate. Having been awarded his Royal Aero Club Certificate in February 1913, in April he attended the Central Flying School. Ross was said to have been a brilliant pilot and had taken part in a number of bombing raids over enemy ports. One of the ships on which he had served was HMS *Engadine*, a former Folkestone to Boulogne ferry that had been taken over by the Navy and fitted out to carry the Short Type 184 seaplane. Ross was the son of the Revd R. Peel Ross and grandson of Captain Horatio Ross of Ross Castle in Montrose, so had 'Naval' blood in his family. It was announced in September that Commander Ross was to marry Muriel Kennard, the younger daughter of Mr and Mrs Kennard of Cleveland, Westgate-on-Sea.

It is claimed that Ross was something of a disciplinarian, but that would not have been anything unusual at that time, and he did have a difficult job in organising the station for defence against attacks by Zeppelin and Gotha bombers. Some pilots, however, had some difficulty understanding Westgate's

SQDR. COMDR. CHAS. BUTLER. DSO. DSC

Squadron Commander
C. H. Butler DSC DSO taking
a nap. He was Mentioned in
Despatches on two occasions
for 'Meritorious Work' and
Great Gallantry'. (*Chris Lofft*)

operational role and were confused as to why they were there. They were
not sure whether the station's main operational role was simply to supply
aeroplanes to patrol the Thames Estuary and chase Zeppelins that threatened
to attack London, or to defend the towns of Margate and Ramsgate and
others in the local area from attack.

Squadron Commander Charles Henry Butler was posted to Westgate in
October and was a veteran of the war in the Dardanelles. Butler had learned
to fly at Eastbourne and the Pashley School at Shoreham, where he had been
awarded his Royal Aero Club Certificate, No. 902, on 6 September 1914.
He had joined the RNAS in the same month and in March 1915 was posted
to the Dardanelles with No. 3 Squadron. While there, he had carried out a
number of photographic reconnaissance sorties, often accompanied by Flight
Lieutenant Thomson, who would also later be posted to Manston. In June
1915, Butler was wounded in the right foot and a subsequent infection might
have been the beginning of a number of serious health problems from which
he suffered.

Soon after arriving at Westgate, Butler was plagued by a bad case of
jaundice and cholecystitis, and in November he was admitted to the Royal
Naval Hospital Haslar at Gosport in Hampshire on three separate occasions.
His last bout of illness began on 15 February 1916, when he suffered a case of

recurring enteritis. He was finally declared fully fit for service a few days later, and after being posted to Westgate was appointed as second in command to Squadron Commander Ross.

Ross had become increasingly concerned about the troubled landing ground at Westgate, but it continued to be used and there were further accidents that caused alarm. One such incident occurred on 24 March, when Sub-Lieutenant Bush's Bristol Scout ran off the end of the cliff and crashed onto the beach below. Fortunately the tide was out and, although the machine was totally wrecked, Bush suffered only minor injuries.

There were a number of other incidents that could not be blamed on the landing ground, and forced landings were a regular occurrence, such as that on 14 December when the pilot of Curtiss JN-3 biplane, serial number 3366, had to make an unscheduled landing in a field near Acol. The aeroplane was among a small batch of Canadian-built Curtiss aircraft that were based at both Westgate and Manston, having been built under licence in Britain and including serial numbers 3406, 3447 and 3462. With its Curtiss-built OX-5 V8 90 hp engine, this dual-seat aeroplane allowed the student to sit in the front, with his instructor immediately behind him, and it was considered to be the safest and most able of its type on which to train pilots.

By early 1916, the authorities were also becoming increasingly concerned about the landing ground at Westgate and in March the Divisional Commander of Air Stations at Chatham, Wing Commander Henry Smyth-Osbourne, wrote to His Majesty's Commander-in-Chief of Ships and Vessels. A former cadet of the Britannia Royal Naval College, Smyth-Osbourne had only recently returned to England after serving in the West Indies on board HMS *Cordelia*, on which he was then acting as a Flag Lieutenant. He had served with the Channel Fleet, the China Station, on the Cruiser Squadron and the Mediterranean Fleet. He was an influential figure who had held a number of important posts, including that of Officer in Command of Air Stations under the Commander-in-Chief of the Nore Command.

In his letter, Smyth-Osbourne gave his opinion that the landing ground at Westgate was small and dangerous, and that the portion of the station devoted to landplanes should be transferred to Manston. As a result of his communication, the first piece of land of what was to become known as RAF Manston was purchased. The Treasury acquired some 20 acres of Manston Court Farm, but its initial role was just to serve as an emergency night-landing ground for Westgate.

There is some confusion about a landing ground at a place called Mutrix Farm that was situated on land adjacent to the seaplane base. Thirty-seven acres of Mutrix Farm had been absorbed by the landing ground at Westgate, and they were effectively one and the same place.

CHAPTER 3

RNAS Manston

The area around Thanet and Manston is steeped in history going back many hundreds of years before it became the setting for an airfield. During the Middle Ages, Manston Court was the seat of the rich and influential Manston family, with Richard de Manston holding office under King John and William de Manston being appointed the Sheriff of Kent in 1436. The original spelling of Manston was 'Mannestone', but by the fourteenth century various corruptions had whittled it down to the current spelling and pronunciation. Strangely enough, in 1916, a number of reports from No. 3 Wing RNAS still spelt it 'Manstone'. The discovery of an Anglo-Saxon sword and 200 Roman graves proved that Manston had been the scene of many battles long before the one with which it was later best associated, 'The Battle of Britain'.

The village of Manston that gave the airfield its name is approximately one mile north-west of Ramsgate and is still quite small. The Jolly Farmer public house is at the centre of the community and also has a long history, its first recorded use being as a farm building in 1672, before becoming established as an inn around 1738, when it was called the Jolly Farmers. St Catherine's Church, built in 1872, the war memorial, and the pub are still today the village's most notable features, and with the exception of a small number of modern houses, it has changed very little over the years.

The land on which the airfield was established was vividly described in the *Royal Air Force Journal* as a rolling plain of rapidly ripening crops with a farm cottage here and there nestling amidst the trees. The view to the north-east was of a quaint old farmhouse known as Pouce's Farm, built in the year 1580, and immediately in front of the farmhouse was an historic fourteenth-century barn with massive oak beams. Adjacent to the barn was Rose Cottage, the name of which was subsequently changed to Holmecroft. It later became the traditional residence of the Commanding Officer. On the left of Rose Cottage were three other cottages known as Oakleigh, The Nook, and Mayfield. The latter would become the offices of Station Headquarters. It is ironic that such an idyllic place should later have been the scene of so much death and destruction.

Captain Robert Halley, a pilot at Manston, later recalled the delights of Rose Cottage when it was used as an Officers' Mess after it had been taken over by the Admiralty. Not only was it a delightful billet with wonderful period furniture but he claimed that the food served there was very special. The steward in Rose Cottage, who had apparently previously worked in the House of Commons, was able to obtain and serve such rare dishes as curried prawns and larks' tongues, and Halley considered himself very lucky to be there.

Although the airfield took its name from the village of Manston, there are also close associations with the village of Minster lying just outside the airfield boundary. One reason for that is that the village of Manston does not have its own cemetery, but Minster does and it was often used to inter service personnel from Manston as well as those civilians who came from the local area. The cemetery is at the top of the village just across the road from the modern-day airfield and contains seventy graves of those who died in the First World War. Minster with its ancient abbey is also somewhat larger than Manston, with a number of shops, public houses and its own railway station from where trains run directly to London via Canterbury. Minster may not have the same serene setting as Manston village, but it was and still is a typical English village that would have enthralled visitors who came from overseas.

By February 1916, Manston airfield still comprised nothing more than a few very large wooden packing cases that passed as 'huts', in which airmen such as Leading Air Mechanic Wood spent the night. The huts were equipped with two bunks, a field telephone, and several bowls of oily rags that in an emergency were formed into a letter 'T' and placed on the ground to guide pilots into the wind. The oily rags were then lit so as to guide the pilots to the ground. The first recorded operational landing was on the night of 19 March, when Lieutenant Buss arrived in a B.E.2c biplane, serial number 1159, after taking off from Westgate and engaging in a fruitless sortie in pursuit of an airship.

It is difficult to explain the exact position of the first landing ground to those who are not familiar with the airfield, but it can best be described as an area of ground to the east of the present passenger terminal. It then covered just a quarter of a square mile, with three pieces of ground marked out for three runways and a number of small hangars and huts that had been dismantled at Westgate and then transported to and rebuilt at Manston. Anyone who knows Manston well is aware that the airfield covers a huge area of open ground, and to the south on a clear day there are views of Pegwell Bay and, in the distance, Dover. In 1916, there was plenty of room for development, and it was not long before the airfield began to expand

– the land to the west was built on for the first accommodation.

Squadron Commander R. J. Bone arrived at Manston on Sunday 16 March in a Nieuport from Detling because he claimed that he had noticed there was a pattern in the timing of when German seaplanes had attacked the local area. He did not have too long to wait and, as he had predicted, at lunchtime a number of seaplanes arrived over the coast and proceeded to bomb Margate. After taking off from Manston, Bone chased the enemy planes out to sea as they proceeded back towards the safety of Zeebrugge. Not put off by the prospect of a long flight over the sea, Bone climbed towards them and was finally rewarded when he managed to get underneath one of them and close enough to fire. The German seaplane was hit and damaged enough that its pilot was forced into ditching in the sea. The pilot survived and although the seaplane was later safely towed into Zeebrugge, Bone was still awarded the DSO, the first to be awarded to a pilot from Westgate. He was also later awarded Greece's highest honour, The Order of Redeemer, for his work in the Dardanelles.

Despite the problems with the landing ground at Westgate, aeroplanes continued to be delivered there and on 6 April 1916, two Royal Aircraft Factory B.E.2c biplanes arrived there, one of them serial number 8497. Commander Marix had a photo taken of the occasion that was later turned into a postcard, featuring three aeroplanes parked side by side with a bell tent sitting in what looks like an idyllic setting in front of some trees. The commander appears to be casually dressed in white shirt, jacket and slacks, but in the top left-hand corner of the postcard in a cameo photo, he appears to be dressed more formally in naval uniform.

It was in April 1916 that the move to Manston was officially sanctioned by the Treasury, and the following month No. 3 Wing of the RNAS was the first unit to move into Manston, posted in from Detling. At Detling, the Wing had originally comprised no more than four Curtiss biplanes used for the defence of London. However, by the time it was moved to Manston it was equipped with a number of different types of aeroplane including two BE.2cs, a Short Biplane, a single Curtiss biplane, and four Sopwith 1½ Strutters. The two-seat fighter version of the latter was the first aeroplane to be fitted with interrupter gear to allow its guns to be fired through the arc of its propeller.

Number 3 Wing RNAS had originally been formed as part of an agreement to set up a joint Anglo-French Strategic Bombing Force. It had originally been proposed that aeroplanes based on the South Coast should bomb enemy objectives on the Continent by flying directly from England. When it was realised that they probably did not have the range to reach airfields in France and Belgium, to say nothing about the return journey, it was decided to move the Wing to Manston while arrangements were made for the move to France.

It was noted in the Manston Diary on 29 May that the RNAS station at

Detling had been handed over to the RFC and put on C&M. The telegram from the C-in-C of Nore Command to the Air Division of the Admiralty read simply: 'Detling Air Station reduced to C&M today (29 May 1916) on transfer to Manston.' In the same entry it was noted that the allegedly dangerous landing ground at Westgate was to be closed down because of its unsuitability for night landings. The six aeroplanes that formed the War Flight were moved to Manston, which according to the official records, was described as being merely a small aerodrome with only Bessonneau hangars for accommodation. However, the Admiralty had approved the building of a number of hangars at Manston that were suitable for the maintenance of large bombers.

On 20 May 1916, the last patrol flown from the landing ground at Westgate was made by Flight Lieutenant Butler in pursuit of an enemy aeroplane that had dropped a number of bombs on Broadstairs. Despite his best efforts searching the local area to catch the raider on that final patrol, his sortie proved to be fruitless.

It was noted that Manston had become fully operational on 29 May 1916, but there is some disagreement and misinformation about who was the first Commanding Officer at Manston. A number of documents and publications state that Squadron Commander Reginald Leonard George Marix DSO was the first Commanding Officer, but the Station Diary states that it was Wing Commander Richard Bell-Davies VC, DSO.

Bell-Davies had been commissioned into the Royal Navy in December 1905 as a Sub-Lieutenant. He had been promoted to Lieutenant in 1908, and after training on the first ever course at the Central Flying School, he was awarded his wings in 1914. In April 1915, he had been awarded the DSO for taking part in a daring low-level raid on 23 January, attacking submarine pens at Ostend and Zeebrugge. Later that year he was posted to the Dardanelles and awarded the Victoria Cross (VC) for his actions on 19 November when he landed behind Turkish lines and rescued Flight Sub-Lieutenant Gilbert Formby Smylie. It was real *Boy's Own* stuff, and after Smylie's aeroplane had been shot down, and despite the fact that Turkish forces were closing in on them, Bell-Davies did not hesitate but landed and picked him up. In June 1916, he was promoted to the rank of Lieutenant Commander, which later became the equivalent to the rank of Squadron Leader.

After leaving Manston, Bell-Davies went back to work in various departments in the Admiralty, but he later commanded ships such as HMS *Royal Sovereign*; HMS *Cornwall*, and HMS *Cumberland*. He had married Mary, the daughter of Major-General R. A. Kerr Montgomery in 1920 and they had two children, a son and a daughter. His son, Lancelot Richard Bell-Davies, was born in 1943 and followed in his father's footsteps, also having a distinguished career in the Royal Navy. Bell-Davies had retired in 1941, but was enticed out of retirement to test the aircraft carrier HMS *Pretoria*

Castle that had been converted from a luxury liner. Being the station's first Commanding Officer, it is quite fitting that on the domestic site of former RAF Manston there is a road named after him.

Although Squadron Commander Marix was not the commanding officer of RNAS Manston he was definitely there and acting in the role of the Commanding Officer of No. 3 Wing. That is where the confusion may originate. Marix might have been the Officer Commanding RNAS Manston, rather than Commanding Officer, there being a subtle difference in the titles. The Officer Commanding was the most senior officer in charge, but answered effectively to another superior officer. In the case of Manston, this was probably Bell-Davies, or more likely, Squadron Commander Ross at Westgate because Manston was only a sub station of RNAS Westgate.

Marix was the other officer and pilot who had taken part in the infamous bombing raid on the Düsseldorf Zeppelin sheds along with Spenser Grey in October 1914. On that occasion, Grey's aeroplane had been badly damaged by enemy fire and he had had to make a forced landing some twenty miles away from his base airfield near Antwerp. Being ever resourceful, Grey borrowed a bicycle and rode the last twenty miles back to the airfield at Wilrijk on two wheels!

Commissioned into the Royal Navy as a Sub-Lieutenant in November 1912, Marix had been attached to the Royal Naval Flying School at Eastchurch. He had gained his Royal Aero Club Certificate, No. 403, on 21 January 1913, and in August that year he was posted to the Central Flying School for military instruction. In early 1914, he was promoted to the rank of Lieutenant and soon afterwards he was appointed as a Flight Commander on No. 3 Squadron. On 1 January 1916, he was promoted to the rank of Squadron Commander and had been posted to No. 3 Wing as a Training Officer, which was then still based at Detling.

Soon afterwards, Marix was badly injured in a flying accident in France, when as the Commanding Officer of No. 3 Wing, and as part of the unit's proposed move to France, he had flown there with Flight Sub-Lieutenant Draper. The purpose of their operation was to deliver a pair of Sopwith 1½ Strutters and inspect the airfield where it had been proposed that the Wing would be based. On the way there they called in at an airfield near Paris, where the French asked them if they would like to fly one of their new aeroplanes – an offer they could not refuse. Unfortunately the flight ended with Marix getting into a spin from which he was unable to recover. It resulted in his aeroplane crashing to the ground and he had to have a leg amputated as a result of his injuries.

Manston's second Commanding Officer in the space of a few months was Wing Commander Leslie Elder who had been born on 26 June 1874 and took up that post on 14 June 1916. It is claimed that he was the oldest pilot in the

RNAS, and he was fast approaching his forty-second birthday! He had been awarded his Royal Aero Club Certificate, No. 1681, on 31 August 1915 after training on a Maurice Farman at Chingford. A very experienced naval officer, in January 1915 he had been promoted from Commander to Captain, but had subsequently taken a reduction in rank to Wing Commander (Commander), and despite being new to flying, he was going to play an important role in the organisation of No. 3 Wing.

Despite regular incursions by the Zeppelin airships and Gotha bombers, Manston's War Flight was not established until 27 June 1916, when six aeroplanes, plus pilots and some forty ratings, were transferred from Westgate to Manston under the leadership of Flight Commander Butler. He had recently been awarded the Distinguished Service Cross (DSC) for gallantry in the Dardanelles campaign. The War Flight remained under the overall control of Squadron Commander Robert Peel Ross at Westgate and was tasked with flying inshore and coastal patrols for the defence of Thanet.

Number 3 Wing continued to grow at Manston, but by early June a number of pilots who had acted as flying instructors had already left for France and were based at Luxeuil-les-Bains, 60 miles south of Nancy. On 10 June, one of them – a twenty-eight-year-old Canadian, Sub-Lieutenant George Knox Williams – was killed in a flying accident when his Sopwith 1½ Strutter collided with a French biplane. Williams and the French pilot he was training were killed instantly, as were the two French pilots in the other aeroplane.

Number 3 Wing RNAS was both an operational unit and a training unit, and the latter was probably why it suffered more than its fair share of accidents. Back at Manston there were a number of less serious accidents, and on 12 June, Sopwith 1½ Strutter, serial number 9407 of No. 3 Wing, which had arrived in May, was badly damaged after talking part in a test flight. Another Sopwith was also badly damaged on 7 July, but neither incident involved fatalities.

A huge number of Sopwith 1½ Strutters allocated to the Wing passed through Manston in June, including those with these serial numbers: 9401 on the 8th, 9414 on the 9th, 9652 on the 23rd, and 9408 on the 25th. Numbers 9400, 9401, 9408 and 9414 were transported by road and the first two machines had been transported by road by Oakley's Ltd. They arrived in such a bad condition that it had been necessary to send them back for extensive repairs and they would not return to Manston for some time. When the Battle of the Somme was launched in July, it both delayed the main elements of No. 3 Wing moving over to France and reduced its allocation of aeroplanes. Many of its Sopwith 1½ Strutters had to be handed over to the RFC and were used to carry out long-range reconnaissance.

Later in June, Wing Commander Elder, for obvious reasons known as 'Daddy' Elder, went to France and arranged for the bulk of the unit to move to Luxeuil. By then it was equipped with a large number of various types of aeroplane, including the Short Bomber biplane, which also served with No. 7 Squadron RNAS. Nine of them belonging to No. 3 Wing were similarly temporarily based at Manston while awaiting modifications by the manufacturers to their exhaust systems.

A report sent to Elder stated that the exhaust stubs regularly blew off in the air, but a number of them had blown off on the ground, and it is claimed that the aircraft were totally unreliable. The failure occurred at the joint that connected the exhaust to the extension that carried it up the strut, the primary cause being vibration and the occasional backfire. If the pipe broke, it was a real source of danger because it allowed flames from the exhaust to come into contact with the fuselage. The only remedy was to fit a short length of flexible metallic tubing between the exhaust and the extension, and that work was gradually being out on all the Short Bombers.

Among those laid up at Manston during June and July were serial numbers 9476, 9478, 9480, 9482, 9485, and 9491. To keep No. 7 Squadron up to strength it was re-equipped with more Handley Page O/100s to replace its Short Bombers. Among those languishing at Manston were serial numbers 9634, 9366, and 9368. Numbers 9369 and 9370 arrived at Manston in January 1917, and with their single Rolls-Royce Eagle or Sunbeam engine powering a two-bladed propeller they were dreadfully underpowered.

CHAPTER 4

The French Connection

In May 1916, the War Flight at Manston is mentioned for the first time, and the records state that because of the demise of the landing ground at Westgate the six aeroplanes should be moved to Manston. Flight Commander Butler DSC, DSO took over command of the flight, which remained largely inactive for many months.

The first substantial element of No. 3 Wing moved out from Manston to France on 16 June, the party consisting of a single officer and 125 men from the ranks, who were sent to develop a new airfield at Luxeuil, as mentioned in the previous chapter. The Wing flew its first operational sorties on 30 July when nine aeroplanes attacked a benzene store near Mülheim, the combined Anglo-French force consisting of four French Farmans, one Sopwith, and a single Nieuport. The British contingent was made up of two Sopwith bombers (modified single-seat Sopwith 1½ Strutters) and a single Sopwith fighter for protection. One of the RNAS Sopwith bombers damaged its propeller on take-off and was unable to take part in the raid, which otherwise was considered to be a success.

Very few documents describe the exact make-up of No. 3 Wing, but a letter written in July 1916 from the Air Department to the Commanding Officer of the Wing states that it consisted of five squadrons. The first unit was No. 3 Squadron and its personnel were scheduled to arrive at Manston by 15 July. After it had moved out to France, more personnel and machines would arrive at Manston to form No. 4 Squadron. Following its move to France, the pattern would continue with further personnel and machines arriving at Manston to make up the fifth unit that would follow the others out to France.

The normal procedure for No. 3 Wing to accept an aeroplane was that when a machine was ready to collect, normally from the Isle of Grain, the Admiralty would notify the Wing and a pilot would immediately be dispatched to fly it to Manston. Its guns, bombing gear and compass were thoroughly tested before the machines were flown to France in groups of two or three. There were strict orders demanding that when an aeroplane left Manston its guns had to be working and ready for immediate action in case the crew should encounter enemy machines along the way.

The aeroplanes were normally flown from Manston to Le Bourget aerodrome near Paris and, on arrival, pilots reported to Squadron Commander Courtney of the Naval Air Station Paris. He issued the final instructions to crews who were delivering the machines to No. 3 Wing's base, but he demanded to be given 24 hours' notice of such movements before the machines departed from Manston. Flight Lieutenant Thomson was in command of operations at Manston and was ordered to remain there until all parties had departed for France or until such time that he was relieved.

For those parties travelling to France by road, rail and sea, which was mainly those airmen in the ranks, their officers or Senior NCO had to apply to the Director of Air Services to organise transport for them between Manston and Vessoul in France. Four days before their departure a telegram had to be sent to Squadron Commander Courtney, informing him of their time and date of departure and arrival at Le Havre. Their normal route was via the ports of Southampton and Le Havre, meals and other provisions being supplied by the Duty Naval Transport Officer at Southampton. In France, the Naval Assistant at Le Havre, Lieutenant Norton, was responsible. Courtney had overall responsibility for arrangements concerning meals and transport as far as Paris, and also acted as the liaison officer with the Commanding Officer of No. 3 Wing.

Wing Commander Elder's deadline for the Wing to complete its move to France was 1 October, having ordered that all stores should be removed from Manston and sent to France by that date. After that date, the Stores Officer was ordered to close his books and transfer all his accounts to No. 3 Wing in France.

The Engineering Officer, Lieutenant Commander Samson, who had been one of the first airmen to land in Thanet in April 1912, was also ordered to remain at Manston until it closed and then report to the Admiralty for further instructions. Since what probably seemed like those distant days of 1912, Samson had been awarded the DSO for carrying out what was the very first night bombing mission in history, on 14 December 1914. It was all the more remarkable because he carried it out by flying a Maurice Farman aeroplane, a slow and unwieldy type that would soon be relegated to the training role.

The Manston War Flight went into action for the first time on 9 July after a warning from the look-out at the North Foreland who had heard the sound of aeroplane engines approaching from the sea. Flight Sub-Lieutenant Greig searched the area for over an hour but failed to catch sight of enemy machines, although his colleague Flight Sub-Lieutenant Mills, who had taken off five minutes after Greig, soon spotted the intruder. Mills slowly climbed up to 12,000 feet and got into position only a few hundred yards behind the enemy machine, but despite firing all his ammunition and flying half way to Ostend in the process of the pursuit, Mills was forced to turn back without any confirmation that the enemy had even been hit let alone damaged. Several other pilots were involved in the chase, but none of them were any more successful than Mills, including the future AOC of Fighter Command, Sholto Douglas. At the time of the incident, Sholto Douglas was just a Flight Lieutenant.

On 23 July, Squadron Commander Marix sent another detailed and lengthy report about the state of some of the Sopwiths and the Shorts to Elder, who it seems was still in command of Manston, although he had flown out to Luxeuil. It did not exactly portray British engineering in a good light, and it is worth detailing the whole of the report, as it explains much of what was going on at RNAS Manston at that time.

Marix's report highlighted a number of failures in key components, causing considerable delays in sending machines to France. Various machines were affected, but particularly those Sopwiths numbered 9400, 9401, 9408 and 9414, and those from 9400 were having to have new engines fitted. He reported that 9414 was serviceable, while the other two aeroplanes had been sent back to the contractors, Oakley's, where they were being repaired. It was stated that when they did eventually return to Manston, spare engines would have to be fitted to them because those originally built into the airframe required spare parts that were not available at Manston. It had also been discovered that in the British-built engines, up to and including No. 284, the screws retaining the gudgeon pins were not strong enough, leading to engine failures on a number of occasions. Although new screws were available, it was considered inadvisable to allow those machines with British-built engines to proceed to France. The engines had been taken away for the screws to be replaced and a number of pistons were also sent off for inspection. They were transported to London by Warrant Officer English and were returned to Manston the following week.

It was emphasised that all those British-built Clerget engines numbered above 284, and all French-built engines, should not be affected, but trouble could be expected from those numbered below 284. Two other Sopwiths, 9706 and 9709, had also been allocated to No. 3 Wing, but because a large Army order was taking precedence over the requirements of those being built for the RNAS, they were not expected to arrive at Manston for some time.

Of the individual machines, Elder stated that Sopwith 9654, a long-distance fighter version, was ready to leave for France as soon as new screws had been fitted. Number 9664 had remained at Manston for a new bomb sight to be fitted and for trials to be carried out, but that had now been done and the machine would proceed to France as soon as its engine had been reassembled with new screws.

Sopwith 9670 had been damaged at Manston when landing after a flight from Brooklands, but repairs had been under way and Marix claimed that it was expected to be serviceable within a few days. Machine number 9673 was listed as an 'Analite bomb dropper' that had been sent to Manston for trials, but it was stated that these had been unsatisfactory and that the bomb dropping gear needed to be worked on. All the bombs could not be fitted on to the racks, the release gear needed changing, and it had been flown to the Isle of Grain. It was estimated that the work would take at least fourteen days.

One machine that had undergone repairs by Fairey Engineering was 9407, which was described as being in flying order and should have been sent to France in place of 9414 as a fighter. Because Faireys had not equipped it with synchronising gear, arrangements had to be made with the Admiralty to have it flown to the Isle of Grain instead, where it was to be fitted out within a week. Commander Holland had supplied a Scarff mounting for the guns on 9654, and hoped to get another set for 9407 by the time it had been fitted with the synchronising gear.

On page 3 of his report, Marix turned his attention to the Short aeroplanes of which nine were still at Manston awaiting repairs to their exhaust systems. Despite the fact that Marix had demanded that he should be given the tubing and acetylene welding equipment to do the job, it had still not arrived at Manston. Not all of the aeroplanes had been manufactured by Shorts, serial numbers 9478, 9480, 9481 and 9482 having been built by Mann Egerton of Norwich. Founded in 1905 by Gerald Mann, it had previously been involved in the production of motor cars, but during the Great War it was also producing aeroplanes. Altogether it built twenty Short Bombers, but also built and designed two types of its own – Types 'B' and 'H'.

Of the individual aeroplanes, Elder reported that 9310 was complete except for the problem with its exhaust system and fittings. As regards 9308, it had a number of problems including the fact that no fuse wire had been fitted to the bomb frame and no forward window had been put in for the bomb sight. Machines 9311, 9312 and 9314 were serviceable and other Short Brothers-built machines were ready to leave Manston as soon as their exhaust pipes had been altered and fusing wire fitted to 9308.

Those machines built by Mann Egerton were not ready, but workmen from the company had arrived at Manston and were carrying out the necessary work to the bomb racks. The bomb sight of 9478 had been broken, but another one was on order to replace it, and there were only two bomb frames on each wing so others were on their way to Manston. The machine had not been wired up properly, no fuse wire was fitted, and there was no gun mounting. The carbon brush in the magnets was broken and one was being made on site, but just to add to the long list of repairs, the machine had been in a collision and the wing extension had been damaged. By comparison, the repairs needed to 9480 were relatively simple, it only needing wire to be fitted to the bomb release mechanism, and the dropping levers fitted.

Number 9481 also needed lengthy repairs, and it had no fuse wire fitted or wire fitted to the bomb release mechanism. It had no gun mounting and there were serious problems with the fuselage, particularly with the nuts and bolts that supported the bracing. Marix considered that to be a serious problem and said he would ensure that other machines were examined to confirm that similar fittings were safe on them.

The final machine mentioned in Marix's report was Short 9481, and he explained that experiments had been carried out with that aeroplane in order to find out whether the engine was capable of slow running in the air. He said that had not been possible with any other machine, but Samson's experiments had been very successful and would be completed in a few days' time, and a report would be forwarded to the Admiralty. There were a few problems with the machine: it was not fitted with fusing wire or wired for releasing bombs, and there was no gun mounting fitted.

Marix completed his report by stating that the machines built by the Mann Egerton company were at best incomplete, and gun mountings were not fitted or available except for 9480. The company's workmen were on site at Manston and attending to the fusing and bomb releasing gear. They were also fitting new clips to hold the bomb racks in place, based on the pattern of those produced by Shorts, because those currently fitted interfered with the fusing rods.

In July, the first of the twenty-eight HP O/100 bombers ordered for the RNAS began to arrive at Manston where a new facility and organisation had been set up. This was the Handley Page Training Flight, which was established to train both air and ground crews and to prepare the aircraft for operational service in France. The aircraft, powered by two Roll-Royce Eagle engines that gave it a top speed of 97 mph, had a crew of four and could carry a 454 kg bomb load.

The aircraft were manufactured at the Handley Page factory in Cricklewood and assembled at another workshop in Kinsgbury before being towed to Hendon. There they underwent final assembly before being test flown and delivered to Manston where they were fitted out for operational service in France with additional equipment such as bombing gear and machine guns. Among those HP O/100s that passed through Manston during 1916 were numbers 1457, 1458, 1459 and 1461, all of which were destined for service with No. 3 Wing. It was also to train both air and ground crews on the aircraft, and it was commanded by recently promoted Squadron Commander Gordon Lindsay Thomson DSC, who was already acting as Stores Officer for the Wing.

Born in Wandsworth, London, Thomson, who was soon to become the Commanding Officer of Manston, was probably the most successful sportsman of all those who held the post of Commanding Officer at Manston. Having been educated at University College School, Hampstead, and Trinity Hall, Cambridge, he excelled as a rower and at the Olympic Games in 1908 he partnered John Fenning to win the gold medal in the coxless pairs. In the same Games he also won a silver medal in the coxless fours, and the following year he rowed for Cambridge in the annual boat race. In 1910, he became a Cambridge 'Blue'. He also excelled at rugby, playing for the University College School Old Boys, London Scottish, and Surrey.

At the outbreak of war, Thomson had given up a sporting career and joined the RNAS, learning to fly at the Bristol Flying School at Brooklands where he was awarded the Royal Aero Club Certificate No. 873 on 20 August 1914. Soon afterwards he was posted to Gallipoli where he became exceptionally talented at flying low-level photographic reconnaissance sorties, often accompanied by Flight Lieutenant Butler of the Manston War Flight.

On 16 March 1916, it had been announced by the Admiralty that both officers were to be awarded the DSC. The citation, covering both officers, states, 'These two pilots have carried out photographic work on many occasions flying at low altitude over the enemy's lines to get good results.' It is fitting that both were posted to Manston where they were able to use their skill and experience and to continue their friendship.

The former Commanding Officer of Westgate, Squadron Commander Babington, was put in command of what became known as the Handley Page squadron, an offshoot of the Training Flight that was preparing to move to France. It was fitting that he should command the flight, as he had been the first pilot to fly the type O/100, 1455, when it had been tested on 18 December 1915. The original establishment for the Handley Page squadrons was set at eighteen aeroplanes per unit, with ten O/100s in one flight and another eight in the other, but when that establishment was changed to ten, eight were sent over to the other side of the airfield to form a separate unit, No. 7A Squadron.

Number 3 Wing lost another pilot and aeroplane on 20 July when Flight Sub-Lieutenant Douglas H. Whittier crashed after trying to perform a loop in a Bristol Scout, serial number C1245. A report to Wing Commander Elder claimed that Whittier attempted the loop from only 1,500 feet and that the machine then had side-slipped before it had nosedived to the ground before the pilot had any chance to regain control. Whittier, a twenty-four-year-old Canadian, was the son of Anson Dudley and Amelia of St Ann Street, Victoria, British Columbia, and was buried in Minster Cemetery, just a short distance across the airfield.

On 30 July 1916, Flight Sub-Lieutenant Butterworth was flying to France when the engine of his Short Bomber, 9312, suddenly seized up and he had to make a forced landing in a large garden of a property on the outskirts of

Paris. Fortunately Butterworth was not badly injured. The main damage to the aeroplane was to its undercarriage, but after being repaired on site it was able to continue its journey to Luxeuil on 11 August.

Problems with the Sopwith machines continued to plague No. 3 Wing and, on 15 September, Elder wrote another long letter to his Commanding Officer in France explaining the reasons for delays in sending them. He said that the delay had been caused by the defective rocker arms on the British-built Clerget engines. Of the last six engines delivered, a rocker arm had broken on each one, and owing to the gross unsuitability of the engines the machines had to stay at Manston. He admitted that he was aware that the Admiralty were designing a new type of rocker arm and that three sets of those had already arrived at Manston.

Because of the number of defects, it had been necessary to open up all the British-built engines on their arrival and very serious defects had been found in nearly every one. In the last two engines more serious problems had been discovered, and it just happened that the Inspecting Engineer was present at that time. He condemned them outright and took some of the defective parts to London with him.

Despite Elder making very strong representations to 'E' Department in the Admiralty, Samson had been informed that they did not think that they had time to send anyone down to Manston to see what state the engines were in. The necessary work to remedy the faults was under way and there were sufficient spare parts to complete the defective engines. Not only were there problems with the engines of the Sopwiths but in a number of cases with the rigging as well, and on at least one occasion it had been found necessary to 'true up' the fuselage of a brand new Sopwith. That was 9730, and Elder stated that he personally intended flying that machine to France.

The Wing Commander confirmed that he currently still had twelve Sopwiths at Manston, four of which belonged to the Naval Flying School – 9400, 9401, 9408, and 9414 (War Flight). Numbers 9401 and 9408 that had been sent back to Oakley's Transport for repairs had not even arrived back at Manston and could not be expected for some time; 9407 had been damaged during a landing after a test flight; and 9722 was among those that had a defective engine. He also urgently requested that a flight lieutenant or flight commander should be posted to Manston to relieve Flight Commander Draper and Flight Lieutenant Newberry, because Flight Commander Thomson was not able to continue on his own once the other two officers had departed for France. It was a very bad state of affairs, and Elder obviously felt quite frustrated by the situation and seemingly his lack of support.

Among those Sopwith 1½ Strutters that passed through and actually left Manston for France was the presentation machine 9739, named *Britons in Egypt No. 2* and described as a fighter. The aeroplane had arrived at Manston on 28 August and departed for Luxeuil on 22 September to join the Sopwith Flight of No. 3 Wing. It was shot down in January 1917. Air Mechanic Fraser was killed instantly, while the pilot, Flight Sub-Lieutenant Smith, was taken prisoner and later died of his injuries.

On 20 September 1916, the Wing lost another pilot when Flight Sub-Lieutenant Scott crashed and was killed, along with his passenger, Air Mechanic 2nd Class F. W. G. Taylor. It is unclear what happened, but they were flying a Sopwith 1½ Strutter when Scott lost control and it crashed to the ground. Twenty-seven-year-old James Douglass Scott was another Canadian, from Montreal, and was buried at Luxeuil. Twenty-three-year-old Frederick William George Taylor from Swindon was also buried at Luxeuil. The final elements of No. 3 Wing moved out in October, although there were a lot of movements of both aeroplanes and airmen backwards and forwards across the English Channel.

As No. 7A Squadron was preparing to move to France, the first of the HP O/100s into service, 1460, arrived at Manston on 1 October and remained there until the 26th when it left for Villacoublay with Squadron Commander Babington at the controls. It arrived there safely, but on taking off from there for Luxeuil it made a forced landing just after take-off and was not made serviceable again until 18 December. The second HP O/100 to be flown to France was 1459, also under Babington's command, on 4 November 1916. On the 21st it moved across the water to France and to its new base at Luxeuil.

The final main elements of No. 3 Wing, comprising Sopwiths and Short Bombers, finally departed for Luxeuil on 14 October under the command of Wing Commander Elder. That was effectively two weeks later than the deadline he had set. The move left Lieutenant Commander Samson effectively redundant and, as previously ordered, he reported to the Admiralty in London to find out what it had in store for him. He may have been a bit surprised to discover that he was being posted overseas and was going to Gallipoli with an element of No. 3 Wing under his command. Over the next twelve months he served not only in that theatre but also in Palestine and the Red Sea on what was described as 'Special Service'. He returned to the Home Establishment in November 1917 and was given command of the Royal Naval Air Station at Great Yarmouth.

Originally, and as had been planned for No. 3 Wing, it had been expected that the HP O/100 bombers would fly directly from Manston to carry out attacks on objectives along the coast of Belgium. That would have been perfectly feasible as far as the aeroplane's range was concerned, but the plan fell foul of bureaucracy. The RNAS station at Manston was in Nore Command, but the aircraft across the Channel were under the control of Dover Command.

The HP O/100 entered service with No. 7 Squadron RNAS, whose first operation had been flown on the night of 15 November 1916 against objectives at Ostend. As a result, the single-engine Short Bomber, with neither the range nor the capability to deliver the loads that were needed, began to be surplus to requirements.

Although the landing ground at Westgate had closed down, the seaplane base was still active and its pilots were involved in a number of incidents such as that on the night of 27–28 November when Flight Sub-Lieutenant Tees suffered engine failure out at sea and had to make an emergency landing by the Tongue light vessel. Fortunately he was able to taxi across and tie up to the vessel, and the Sopwith seaplane, serial number 8146, was towed back to Westgate the following morning. That was the night of the first air raid on London by an aeroplane (Gotha) rather than an airship. Three aeroplanes from the Manston War Flight were sent up in an attempt to catch the lone raider but had no success at all. One of them, flown by Flight Sub-Lieutenant Carr, had to make a forced landing near Sandwich.

A couple of weeks later, on 10 December 1916, Short 184 floatplane 9154 nosedived and crashed into the sea from a considerable height, killing its two crew – Flight Lieutenant John Douglas Hume DSC, from Buckhaven, Fife, and Chief Petty Officer 2nd Class Walter Edwin Bradley DSM. Both were buried on the Isle of Sheppey. Hume, who had celebrated his twentieth birthday just over a month before he was so tragically killed, had joined the RNAS in May 1915 and trained at what was the very first seaplane base on Lake Windermere. From there he had been posted to Hendon and then the Navigation Training School in Portsmouth, before going on to his first operational posting at Calshot. In January, he had sailed out to Mesopotamia on the SS *Huntscastle* and served with 'D' Force, which on one occasion dropped food parcels to British troops who were besieged by Turkish forces. He had returned to England in July and was posted to Westgate, from where, being a prolific letter writer, he had written his last letter to his parents only two days before his death.

It was Squadron Commander Berry who had the difficult task of writing to the parents of Hume and Bradley. In the letter to Hume's family, dated 23 December, he said that he knew their son quite well, having met him at a dance in the Queen's Hotel the night before, when he appeared to be happy and cheerful. He said that he had also spoken to him just before he took off on the fatal sortie and that everything appeared to be well. Berry made a reference to a cut on Hume's trousers that he claimed had happened when the aeroplane had crashed, and said that in his opinion both men would have been unconscious before they hit the water. He also told the parents that after Hume's body had been recovered it had been taken to Sheerness.

There was no mention in Berry's letter of what had caused Hume's aeroplane to crash, but it was later suspected that they had been victims of 'friendly fire', having been fired upon by guns in the Thames Estuary. What evidence there was for such a statement being made is not known and has never been confirmed. Hume was buried on 13 December at Eastminster Cemetery at Sheerness and on 17 May 1918 he was posthumously awarded the DSC.

The local newspapers were keen to report not only on those events that were directly associated with the greater war effort but also on those servicemen who had connections with the local area. On 6 December 1916, the *East Kent Times* reported that Lieutenant Edward Laston Pulling, who for many years was engaged in wireless telegraphy at the North Foreland station, had been awarded the DSC after he had been credited with the destruction of Zeppelin L21 near Great Yarmouth on the morning of 28 November. Pulling was well known both at Manston and in the local area because he had married a local woman, Miss Phyllis Aimee Ross, the only daughter of Lieutenant and Mrs N. Ross of Pierremont Hall School, Broadstairs. Unfortunately, a few weeks later, Pulling made the news again when on 2 March he was killed while flying a B.E.2c near Great Yarmouth, which broke up in the air when he was performing a loop. Twenty-seven-year-old Pulling, from Sidcup, was buried in the cemetery at Great Yarmouth.

At the end of December 1916, the command of RNAS Manston changed again, because by that time Elder, who had been promoted to the rank of Wing Captain, had departed for France with No. 3 Wing. The difference between a wing commander and a wing captain in the RNAS was that the latter had to have experience of being a captain at sea to attain that rank. As we have already noted, the new Commanding Officer of Manston was Gordon Lindsay Thomson DSC, who was also in Command of the Handley Page Training Flight. Other promotions included that of Squadron Commander Ross, who was promoted to Wing Commander, and Flight Lieutenant Butler to Squadron Commander.

CHAPTER 5

1917: The War Flight
In Action

Of all the HP O/100s that were ferried from Manston to France, there is an interesting story about one that did not quite make it to its intended unit. Number 1463, named *Le Amazon*, arrived at Manston on 1 December 1916. On Christmas Day, after being fitted with bombing gear, Lewis guns and other equipment, 1463 was due to leave for France along with another HP O/100, 1462, which had been at Manston since 6 November. However, the departure of these machines on the 25th was further delayed because of engine trouble.

Exactly one month after arriving at Manston, 1463 finally took off on the morning of 1 January 1917 for delivery to the 5th Naval Wing at Dunkirk, accompanied by Sub-Lieutenant Sands in 1462. They were respectively only the third and fourth HP O/100s to be delivered to France. They left Manston within fiften minutes of one another, but both pilots encountered thick, unbroken cloud all the way across the English Channel. Sands found Villacoublay by using dead reckoning, but Flight Lieutenant Henry Connell Vereker, in cloud and experiencing a problem with his compass, was forced to descend as low as 200 feet in an attempt to fix his position. Vereker was running short of fuel when he saw a church spire and then, through a gap in the cloud, spotted an airfield below and landed to find out where he was.

Once on the ground, the crew left the aircraft but almost straightaway realised they had made a mistake. They had landed behind enemy lines, so they began to run back to the aircraft to take off again, but it was too late. With enemy infantry chasing him across the airfield, Vereker almost made it but was caught and dragged off the ladder in the entrance into the aircraft. He was soon to learn that the airfield where he had landed was Chalandry near Laon, some twelve miles behind enemy lines, and was occupied by the German Air Service, being the home base of Flieger Abteilung 208. Vereker and the other four airmen on board – Lieutenant S. R. Hubbard, Leading Mechanics Kennedy and Wright, and Air Mechanic 1st Class Wrigby – were all taken as prisoners of war. As the first HP O/100 was not lost to enemy action until 25

April, it was quite a coup for the Germans to have in their possession one of the latest British bombers intact.

To his credit, when the Germans asked Vereker to fly the aircraft to another airfield he refused to do so, and the Germans were forced to dismantle the bomber. They then took it by road to an airfield at Johannisthal where it was put back together and every detail was examined. Having been reassembled and put back in flying condition, it was later demonstrated and paraded in Essen for Kaiser Wilhelm II. Among other things it was even claimed that at some point the German ace Manfred von Richthofen flew the aircraft, but that was just a rumour. The bomber was flown and tested until August when, due to the carelessness of a German rigger, it crashed and killed all those on board. The rigger had incorrectly connected the ailerons, causing the controls to be reversed, so the bomber went out of control and crashed immediately after taking off.

Born in Langport, Somerset, Vereker was an experienced pilot who had learned to fly at Chingford on the Maurice Farman Longhorn and had been awarded Royal Aero Club Certificate No. 1455 on 21 July 1915. The only other blemish on his service record involved an incident that occurred on 3 April 1916. Then holding the rank of Flight Sub-Lieutenant and while flying Bristol Scout 3029, he had been involved in an accident at Redcar. The aeroplane was written off as a result of a heavy landing, but such things were not uncommon and the incident does not appear to have damaged his service career too much.

In December 1919, and while he was still a prisoner of war, Vereker was mentioned in reports for providing 'valuable service'. What that service was, while he was still being held in captivity, is open to one's imagination! Although he was later put on the Retired List for a while, in 1943 he was recalled to active service and he rose in the ranks to wing commander. It was a rank that he held until his retirement from the service in February 1954.

After the incident involving Vereker's captured machine, no more HP O/100s were flown from Manston to France until April, and there is an interesting follow-up to this incident. During the early hours of 16 March, some six weeks after the Germans had captured the Handley Page bomber, two large aircraft that were thought to be German passed over North Foreland at very low altitude. At least one of them was an enemy machine and it dropped a number of bombs over Margate, Garlinge and Dent de Lion as well as on the piece of the airfield at Mutrix Farm, Westgate. However, there was some doubt about the identity of the second aircraft, and it was later claimed that both of them were enemy machines and that the second aircraft was the very same Handley Page bomber that had been captured by the Germans a few weeks before.

THE "BLACK CAT"

Above: An excellent view of a Handley Page 0/100 bomber running up its engines. Note the 'Black Cat' painted on the nose. (*Chris Lofft*)

Right and next page: Three photos of the Vickers' 40-mm 2-lb 'Pom Pom' gun that defended Manston. The 'Gallant' crew seems to comprise of a number of naval officers posing with the gun while the ratings who actually manned the gun stand in the background. (*Chris Lofft*)

"POM-POM"
MANSTON
. 1917.

A policeman was among those who witnessed the raid and claimed that one of the enemy machines was a Handley Page bomber, but there were a number of other people who also claimed to have identified it as such, and the only ones who did not see it were the look-outs on duty! The HP O/100 was a familiar sight over Thanet and although the official report did claim that the enemy machine could have been the captured British machine, that has never been confirmed.

On the same day, a Sopwith Triplane of the War Flight made one of its first sorties in pursuit of the said aircraft when Squadron Commander Thomson flew N5424 in support of Squadron Commander Butler of the War Flight in the Camel 8951. The Triplane had not long been introduced into service and was gradually replacing the Camels of the RNAS, which were being handed over to the RFC. With its 130 hp Clerget 9B rotary engine, the Triplane was capable of 113 mph and it had an exceptional rate of climb of 1,200 feet per minute, but its only firepower was a single Vickers .303 machine gun. It was also quite fragile, and a number of them were reported as being unable to recover from a steep dive and breaking up in the air.

In February, the Manston War Flight was ordered to provide two aeroplanes to patrol the area between Manston and Whitstable. Also as a consequence of the revised distribution of aeroplanes used for Home Defence, the number of machines that the War Flight could allocate for patrols during daylight was increased to three. There were three main areas that were to be patrolled: (a) Foreness, Manston and Westgate; (b) Foreness and Herne Bay; and (c) Foreness and Deal.

On 13 March 1917, Short Seaplane 9058 was on a local flight involving a sea firing exercise when it was seen to plunge into the sea just off the coast near Cliftonville. The pilot was Flight Sub-Lieutenant Rowland Birks and also on board was a naval armourer, Leading Air Mechanic Ernest Rawson. Despite the fact that a motor launch was sent out immediately, neither airman survived and they are both buried in Margate Cemetery.

The War School's role was to train pilots in all aspects of aerial warfare, but it also supported the Handley Page Training Flight by training pilots to fly the O/100. It was also re-equipped with Sopwith 1½ Strutters, and among those allocated to the school were N5153, N5162, N5109, and N5174 named *Will O' The Wisp*. Sopwith Pups began to arrive at Manston at the end of the year: B5991, B5992, B5993 and B5994 in October, while B5930, B5938, B5958, B5959 and B5960 were delivered in November.

In March, 'Operation X' was activated by the Manston War Flight consisting of three Sopwith Triplanes, three Camels and a Pup made up into three flights. It was to be at a state of readiness from before dawn and until dusk, and the first flight was to cover the area from Manston to Burnham-on-Crouch flying at 10,000 feet The second flight was ordered to take off as soon as the first flight had left the ground and patrol over Manston at 15,000 feet The third flight had to be at an immediate state of readiness and when required it would join the second flight, but it was not to fly further than 5 miles away from the airfield unless in contact with the enemy.

The RFC took over the airfield at Detling at the beginning of April and despite the fact that it had earlier been reduced to C&M, it was still active. There were still three machines of the RNAS based there, and they were transferred to Manston to increase the strength of the War Flight to nine machines.

Also in April, a part of the Royal Naval Flying School at Eastchurch moved to Manston under the Command of Squadron Commander R. H. Jones and the establishment was renamed the War School. The unit was based on the eastern side of the airfield, close to the road that leads to Manston village and Ramsgate. It was allocated two dedicated instructors and equipped with a mixed bag of Maurice Farmans, Avro 504s and later a small number of DH.6s.

On 19 April, a strange and remarkable incident occurred in Ramsgate Harbour that was covered in detail by the *East Kent Times*. During the early morning, an enemy seaplane was observed flying off the coast across Pegwell Bay at about 500 feet. There was some confusion to begin with as to whether it actually was an enemy machine or a friendly one, because it was flying so low and so close to the shore. However, when the seaplane dropped a torpedo it suddenly became quite clear that it was an enemy machine. The weapon, which had been rather unusually connected between the aeroplane's floats, ran swiftly towards the mouth of the harbour. Fortunately the torpedo failed to hit anything and it just ran into a mud bank where it was brought to a sudden halt. It seemed to those who witnessed the incident that immediately after it had dropped the torpedo, the enemy seaplane had developed some kind of trouble. It appeared to be out of control and only narrowly missed hitting the East Pier before it descended and landed on the water just about 100 yards off the sands.

To the amazement of those who witnessed the scene, the German pilot then calmly got out of his machine, made some adjustments to the engine, and then took off again, dropping a couple of small bombs as he climbed into the air. The incident happened before any patrol boat or cutter could approach the seaplane, and as it passed over the East Cliff it was so low that both the pilot and observer could be seen quite clearly. Gunner Ratcliff later waded into the water and disarmed the torpedo, an act for which he was awarded the MBE, but it took some time for those responsible for the defence of the town to come to terms with such an embarrassing situation and explain why a German machine and its crew were allowed to escape so easily.

Squadron Commander Thomsons' tenure as the Commanding Officer of RNAS Manston did not last long, and in May he handed over to Squadron

Commander Babington, who had only recently returned from France. Babington was still closely connected to the Handley Page Flight and in his records it is noted that he was the Officer Commanding RNAS Manston and not the Commanding Officer. He was still on the strength of No. 7 Squadron based in France, and it appears that he was spending half his time at Manston and the other half in France.

Babington was posted to Manston from No. 3 Wing in France and took over command of the Handley Page Training Flight from Thomson. The establishment of the organisation was increased to one Squadron Commander, three Flight Lieutenants, one Flight Sub-Lieutenant, one Lieutenant, one Warrant Officer, and fifty Probationary Flight Officers under instruction.

The first daylight raid by German heavy bombers took place on 25 May 1917. The aeroplane involved, the Gotha, was a large twin-engine bomber that took its name from the company that produced it – Gothaer Waggonfabrik. Carrying a crew of three, its two 260 hp Mercedes in-line engines gave it a maximum speed of 140 mph. It could fly as high as 21,000 feet, carry 1,000 lb of bombs, and had a range of over 500 miles, so Kent and London were well within its range.

The following day, Ramsgate was shaken by a huge explosion that had nothing directly to do with the Germans when the torpedo boat TB4 exploded in the harbour. The disaster happened at 8.15 a.m. when a torpedo was accidentally fired in the wrong tube, killing fourteen ratings. The sound of the explosion was heard on the airfield at Manston, and locally there was complete devastation. All the windows of buildings and houses on York Terrace, Nelson Crescent and Sion Hill were shattered and a large part of the torpedo boat landed in Albert Street, while other pieces came down in Alpha Road and Clarendon Gardens. Thirteen of the fourteen ratings were buried locally in Ramsgate Cemetery, while Leading Seaman Frederick James Welford was buried in Great Yarmouth. Rather ironically, his wife was living locally in Ramsgate at 11 Denmark Road.

The pilots posted to the War Flight in 1917 were a mixed bag of newly qualified airmen and those who were experienced and had already distinguished themselves. Canadian pilot Flight Sub-Lieutenant Alfred Hartley Lofft, who was one of the former, arrived at Manston in May and was assigned to the War Flight. He had been born at St Mary's, Ontario, in January 1895 and had learned to fly at the Curtiss Flying School in Toronto during the summer of 1916, being awarded Royal Aero Club Certificate No. 3390 on 9 August 1916. After sailing to England in late 1916, he trained at Crystal Palace. From there he was posted to the Naval Flying School at Vendôme in France before completing his fast-track Scout training at Cranwell. From there he was sent to Freiston Shores Gunnery School in Lincolnshire before being posted to Manston.

Flight Sub-Lieutenant Lofft sitting in an Avro 504 at Manston. (*Chris Lofft*)

Flight Sub-Lieutenant Lofft's Sopwith Camel B377, outside the hangar. It was delivered to the Manston War Flight on 16 June 1917 and crashed near Manningtree in Essex on 7 July with Lofft after he had chased a Gotha across the Channel. It was repaired and remained in service until April 1918 when it was burned in France to avoid it being captured. (*Chris Lofft*)

Aerial view of the camp and Naval Flying School sheds at Manston, taken by Flight Sub-Lieutenant Lofft in July 1917. (*Chris Lofft*)

An excellent aerial view of the camp at Manston in a photo taken by Flight Sub-Lieutenant Lofft. It shows the buildings of the War Flight, Handley Page Training Flight and Naval Flying School. (*Chris Lofft*)

An aerial view of the Naval Flying School taken by Sub Flight-Lieutenant Lofft. (*Chris Lofft*)

A ground view of the Naval Flying School that was mainly comprised of bell tents and hangars. (*Chris Lofft*)

Above: Another view across the airfield with the more permanent looking flight sheds in the background. (*Chris Lofft*)

Right: A copy of Sub Flight-Lieutenant Lofft's Aero Certificate, Number 3390, issued by the Federation of Aeronautique International on 9 August 1916. (*Chris Lofft*)

Fédération Aéronautique Internationale
British Empire.

We the undersigned, recognised by the F. A. I. as the sporting authority in the British Empire certify that | Nous soussignés, pouvoir sportif reconnu par la F. A. I. pour l' Empire Britannique certifions que

Alfred Hartley Lofft

Born at St. mary's, on the 22 Jan. 1895, Ont., Canada,

having fulfilled all the conditions stipulated by the F. A. I has been granted an | ayant rempli toutes les conditions imposées par la F A I a été breveté

AVIATOR'S CERTIFICATE.   PILOTE - AVIATEUR.

THE ROYAL AERO CLUB OF THE UNITED KINGDOM.

H C L Holden   V-Chairman.

Secretary.

Date 9 Aug. 1916. N° 3390.

(*Signature of Holder*)

A photograph of Flight Sub-Lieutenant Lofft as it appears on his Aviator's Certificate, bearing the stamp of the Royal Aero Club of the United Kingdom. (*Chris Lofft*)

Flight Sub-Lieutenant Daniel Murray Bayne Galbraith DSC, another Canadian officer, arrived at Manston on 26 June and was also posted to the War Flight. Galbraith had joined the RFC in 1915 and had done his flying training at Chingford before being posted to Cranwell and Dover. He had been awarded the DSC in October 1916 for attacking a large two-seat enemy aeroplane on 28 September. His aeroplane had been badly damaged in the action and he had been wounded, while the enemy machine exploded in the air. Although he was later credited with six enemy machines destroyed, none of them were during his time at Manston. Galbraith remained at Manston until April the following year, when he was posted to Redcar as an instructor.

Another pilot who had already made his mark in the development of both civil and military aviation history was posted to Manston in June, when Lieutenant Frederick Warren Merriam was assigned to the War Flight. He was a very experienced pilot and had made his reputation for his work with the Bristol Aeroplane Company, particularly for the development of the Bristol Boxkite. Despite its name, it was an aeroplane rather than a kite, and early in 1912 he was assured of his place in history when he became the first airman ever to fly through cloud. Having been awarded his Royal Aero Club Certificate, No. 179, on 6 December 1912, Merriam had later been appointed as the Chief Instructor at the Bristol Flying School where he had the reputation of being the finest flying instructor in the country. Commissioned into the RNAS on 27 June 1915, he was posted as an instructor to a number of stations, including Chingford. Daly, Merriam, Lofft, Scott and Butler were among a small number of elite pilots who were good friends and enjoyed each other's company.

The War Flight's plan 'Operation X' was revised and put into effect on 23 June 1917, with orders that Manston should have five Sopwith Triplanes, three Sopwith Camels and a Sopwith Pup at readiness to combat the Gotha threat. The operation was in conjunction with the RNAS station at Eastchurch, which was also ordered to have three Camels at immediate readiness, and this was the first occasion that the Camel was authorised for the purpose of Home Defence.

The first reported success was on Saturday 7 July, when Flight Sub-Lieutenant Scott, in Camel B3774, claimed to have destroyed a Gotha that was 35 miles off the Kent coast. It was one of twenty enemy aircraft that had taken part in an air raid on the capital, and Butler, who had been flying in Camel B3761, was also involved in the action along with several other members of the War Flight. There was, however, some disagreement about who actually shot down the enemy machine – it was also claimed by Lieutenant F. A. D. Grace and Lieutenant G. Murray, both from No. 50 Squadron RFC. The unit

Former employee of the Bristol Aeroplane Company, pioneer aviator and flying instructor Squadron Commander Frederick Warren Merriam during the summer of 1917. (*Chris Lofft*)

The 'Hun'. Four photos of a captured German Albatross being investigated by officers on the ground at Manston. It is understood that this machine was not shot down over England but over France, and it was later sent back to England and toured a number of airfields to allow RFC and RNAS pilots to inspect it. (*Chris Lofft*)

'Looking her over'. (*Chris Lofft*)

'More Hun'. (*Chris Lofft*)

'German Albatross'. (*Chris Lofft*)

was equipped with a number of variants of the B.E.2 and flew from an airfield at Harrietsham near Maidstone, although it had detachments at Bekesbourne, Throwley, and Detling. The accounts of Butler and Scott of the action were later disputed when the GHQ of Home Defence Forces sent the RNAS a copy of what it called a 'tolerably objective account of the 7th July'. It stated, 'It appears more probable from the reports received that it was actually brought down by Lieutenants Grace and Murray, although no doubt the RNAS pilots contributed to its destruction.'

Lofft's log book and a letter that he later wrote home on the 9th give a detailed account and a good insight into the events of the 7th. He noted that he took off on a 'hostile patrol' at 9.32 a.m. in Sopwith Camel B3761, but had to return to Manston after 35 minutes because the pressure system broke down. He then took off again in B3773, and what happened next is best described by him in his own words:

Since the last letter I wrote you I have been doing a lot of flying and I was using Sopwith Triplanes. Then the C.O. gave me a Camel which is the last word in 'fighting scouts'. She resembles a bulldog in appearance, all engine and guns with terrific climbing ability. By the time you get the big rotary engine opened out you are off the ground and go up like an elevator. I don't think it is an exaggeration to say that she is the fastest thing on the planet. Of course, I cannot give you any details, unfortunately, so you will have to draw your own conclusions.

Now for the story of the big air raid on London on the 7th. I had been up since 3.30 a.m. as we were rather expecting something that day (Saturday). The hours went past and at 04.45 when I went for breakfast I was feeling pretty tired. After finishing breakfast I went to my cabin to get a little sleep. I had been lying down for about a quarter of an hour and was just dozing when a scout rushed into the room and told me at once, that the Huns were coming.

I pulled on a pair of boots and made for the machines. Far up in the sky the archies [anti-aircraft fire] were bursting so there wasn't a moment to lose. I scaled my 'Camel' and the mechanics soon had the engine going. They turned me around and I didn't take the time to get into the wind, but went straight off, just missing a Triplane which was taking off in the opposite direction.

I climbed rapidly and at times our anti-aircraft was unpleasantly close. One shell burst underneath me and carried the machine about twenty feet to the right. I went out to sea in the direction of the Huns, but my pressure system gave out and threatened to burst the front tank, so I had to limp back to the aerodrome, my engine eventually cutting out completely.

However, I got down all right and ran for another machine. The Huns by this time, over twenty of them, were well on their way to London, so we waited to get them on their return. Shortly before eleven we were off again, and as soon as we got our height, we saw the beggars far above us going full out for home. At first I flew in formation with several Triplanes, but about thirty miles out to sea we became separated. I gradually drew closer to the Huns, and picked out one white twin-engine 'Gotha' which was getting separated from the rest of the formation, and I 'camped' on his tail as it were. My altimeter showed 17,000 feet and you can take it from me that I was decidedly ill from lack of Oxygen. My engine began dropping revolutions and I nearly wept at the thought of having to give up. However, I managed to get within 400 yards of him, so I let him have several hundred rounds. Some of them went into the machine and he went down.

We were now only a couple of miles from the Dutch coast, so I turned back. I guess the altitude was too much for me and I 'went under', and came out again at 13,500 feet. I felt very ill so I stuffed the nose down to 10,000 feet and went along at that height. My compass was adrift and I had no maps, so after flying for half an hour over the sea without sighting land I began to get a little bit worried. But I kept on and finally sighted the coastline.

Where I was, I did not know, in fact I rather doubted whether it was England or not. My engine was dropping revolutions very quickly and I had only 1,000 feet crossing the coast. The country beneath was very suitable for landing so I 'sogged' along hoping the engine would pick up However, it finally went out altogether , and I did a sharp turn to try and get into a field. Unfortunately, I 'side slipped' as I got a bad bump under one wing and the next thing I knew I was driving towards a house. I was only a few feet from the ground and going like dickens, so I banked sharply and 'hoiked' over a hedge.

As the machine struck the ground on the other side, I saw in front of me a deep brook. The next thing I knew, I was lying underneath the 'crashed' bus with petrol running all over me and seeing thousands of stars. I was able to crawl out after a few minutes, and then a crowd of villagers began to collect as they always do on such occasions.

I was pretty well used up, but the people were kind and gave me something to drink. I found that I was about twenty miles away from Colchester in Essex. They drove me to a telephone and I sent in my report and the Captain of Air Services arranged to have the R.F.C. take the machine away and send a car for me. I got back to the R.F.C. drome in Colchester and a Canadian lieutenant very kindly flew me back to our station. Quite enough excitement for one day, don't you think?

A close-up with the head of Flight Sub-Lieutenant Lofft visible in the cockpit of what appears to be a Sopwith Triplane. (*Chris Lofft*)

The 'bag' for the day for our fellows was one Hun driven down into the sea, two others down in flames and the one I sent down. The Admiralty was greatly 'bucked' over the word and sent us a signal on the performance – the first time on record that they have ever done it. Today the District Captain of the Air Service and a Rear Admiral came to the camp and congratulated us and we were being mentioned in despatches. I had to have a medical examination, but the D.C.A.S. said he would not send the report to the Admiralty, so I will still be in the game. However, I am going to be supported with oxygen tubes after this, so it will be all right.

Despite the counter-claims by the RFC, on 20 July a letter marked 'Secret' from the Admiralty to the Commander-in-Chief of the Nore stated that Squadron Commander Butler was to be awarded the DSO, and Flight Lieutenant John E. Scott and Flight Sub-Lieutenant Rowan H. Daly the DSC. Flight Sub-Lieutenant Alfred H. Lofft was to be 'Mentioned' for his service. The awards were made for their actions during the hostile raid on the 7th and were commanded by the Lords Commissioners of the Admiralty on behalf of the King.

Right: A very smart Flight Sub-Lieutenant Lofft standing in front of a Sopwith Triplane. (*Chris Lofft*)

Below: Described by Flight Sub-Lieutenant Lofft as 'Our fleet of Camels', this is a fine photo of the Manston War Flight with Camel B3842 in the foreground. (*Chris Lofft*)

Flight Sub-Lieutenant Lofft and what he describes as the 'Gang', posing on a Sopwith Triplane. (*Chris Lofft*)

Pilot's of the War Flight at rest and play. Flight Sub-Lieutenant Scott, Harker, DeWilde, Daly and Burt pose for this photo, but it is unclear who's who. Daly is most likely the officer sitting on the step of the flight office. (*Chris Lofft*)

Right: Described in his own words as 'Me in the bus', the head of Flight Sub-Lieutenant Lofft is barely visible in this wonderful photo of the front end of a Sopwith Camel. (*Chris Lofft*)

Below: A copy of Flight Sub-Lieutenant Alfred Hartley Lofft's patrol map. The map covers the Channel and gives the position of each lighthouse and beacon, with the distance and bearing from others around it. Note that although the map dates from 1917, the RNAS station at Manston does not appear. Only Westgate is named on the map but that was the administrative headquarters that controlled Manston.

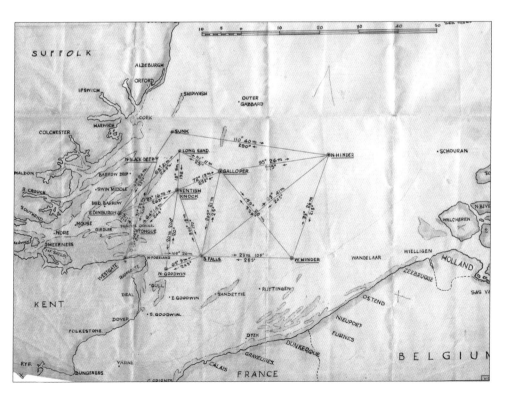

Butler's Camel B3761 had been one of the first to arrive at Manston. It had been delivered to Dover on 5 June, but then diverted to Manston's War Flight on the 19th. On 7 July, Lofft had experienced engine trouble when flying the aeroplane and reported making a bad landing. However, on 12 August, with Butler at the controls, no difficulties were experienced and he attacked a Gotha bomber twenty miles off the coast of North Foreland, but despite firing a total of 420 rounds of ammunition at it, he saw no result.

During August there were a number of Maurice Farman Shorthorns and Longhorns based at Manston, including N6201 and N6202. It was claimed that they were to have been used by the Manston War Flight, but that is very doubtful, and the aged machines could have served in no other role than that of a trainer. Powered by just a single 70 hp Renault engine, the type had been withdrawn from service on the Western Front in 1915.

Despite being thought of as one of the safest aeroplanes on which to train pilots, there were nevertheless a number of accidents involving the type, and one such incident occurred on 2 July when Probationary Flight Officer Harold John Flynn was killed. He was flying in a Maurice Farman MF.7 Longhorn pusher, N5727, when its engine failed and it plunged to the ground from 1,000 feet, killing him instantly. Flynn, another member of the Canadian contingent, was twenty-three years old and from Niagara Falls, Ontario. The son of James and Joanna Flynn was buried in Ramsgate and St Lawrence Cemetery.

Among the HP O/100 bombers that passed through Manston in the months leading up to July or very shortly afterwards were 3117, 3118 and those numbered in the sequence 3123 to 3141. Although most did so without incident, when 3118 landed on 28 July its crew experienced an engine fire and made a heavy landing that broke off the tail skid. Theses machines had flown with 3 Wing in France and had been taken out of service after it had been wound up in April, many of them being handed over to the French Air Service.

Sunday 12 August was a busy day for the Manston War Flight when Flight Commander Sholto Douglas, standing in for Ross, was alerted and sent up a number of Camels, Scouts and Triplanes in search of a lone German raider that had bombed Margate. Eventually all the machines of the War Flight were committed, plus other volunteers such as Squadron Commander Thomson again, who flew in Triplane N535. Among others involved in the action was Flight Sub-Lieutenant DeWilde, flying Camel B3925, who attacked a Gotha off North Foreland without result. His propeller was damaged by enemy fire. Butler, flying in Camel B3761, chased the Gotha half way to Zeebrugge and his machine was hit by an enemy bullet in the engine crankcase. Butler had to give up the chase when one gun ran out of ammunition and the other one jammed.

The aircraft particularly remembered for its action on 22 August was Camel B3834, for some reason named *Wonga Bonga* and flown by Lieutenant Arthur

Right: Flight Sub-Lieutenant Daly sitting in Sopwith Camel number B3834 that was named *Wonga Bonga*. It was delivered to the Manston War Flight on 10 July 1917 and it was flown by Flight Lieutenant A. F. Brandon on 22 August when he shot down a Gotha near Margate. (*Chris Lofft*)

Below: Standing by his Sopwith Camel B3923, 'Springbok' Flight Lieutenant Brandon poses for this photograph. Note the large fur lined gloves that he wearing. (*Peter Oliver*)

Frank Brandon. As he came from South Africa, it might have been assumed that the name had something to do with its wild life, customs, or traditions. However, it has been claimed that the name just referred to the noise made by the Gotha's powerful Mercedes engines.

Thanks to Peter Oliver, we have a copy of Brandon's own account of his action on 22 August. It is interesting that Brandon used the term 'on' a Camel, not in a Camel.

> The best bit of sport I have ever had. I went up at 0930 on a Camel to do a local patrol. I got to 15,000 and found it cold up there, so I decided to come down. When I saw a ground signal put out. 'Readiness'. Keep look out so I climbed like mad to 15,000 feet and saw the rest of my flight coming up to me. Keeping a good look out I saw things that looked like ships in the distance, and on second thought I decided they were the Hun bombing squadron, so I went like hell out to sea so as to get between them and the sun. I was 2,000 above them. When the time came I dived on a big twin-engined Hun, and was sorely tempted to open fire when a long way off, but managed to control myself so decided not to open fire until they did. I got to 200 feet and let her go. When I had fired about 18 rounds I saw the stern gunner drop, and the forward gunner fumbling with his gun, and all the machines round opened on me. I got right to about five yards from the bus and 'cartwheeled' away. I did this three times and the third I nearly ran into it. It came down and crashed about a mile from our aerodrome. I missed it by about four feet as I did this I saw her keel over and burst into flames. The first Hun to land on English soil. When I got hit, and came down, I landed and claimed my Hun and rushed off in another 'Camel' and went after them. When over Ramsgate I saw them coming home. So I followed them up and took quite a while to catch them up. Eventually I met them half way between here and the Scheldt. One was away from the formation and so I attacked him and put about 300 rounds into him, but had no luck. My guns went 'Dud' so I came home with a strong wind against me. All alone over the sea.

Brandon, the third son of Canadian émigré Charles Brandon, was born in Ladysmith and educated in Natal Province before joining the South African Air Force. He had later sailed to England and joined the RNAS on 31 March 1916. Soon afterwards, he was posted overseas to Salonika where he was wounded, and he had been invalided back to the Home Establishment only a short while before, in July 1917.

The actions of Lieutenant Arthur Frank Brandon are not to be confused with those of Lieutenant Alfred de B. Bathe Brandon, who had been credited with the destruction of Zeppelin L15, which crashed off the coast at Margate on the night of 22–23 September 1915 while flying from Hainault in Essex .The Zeppelin may have already been damaged by anti-aircraft fire, but Lieutenant Brandon had used Ranken darts to bring it down.

A. F. Brandon's aeroplane *Wonga Bonga* was powered by a Clerget 9B engine and had been delivered to the War Flight on 10 July. On the day in question, during the air raid on 22 August, Brandon was already airborne and cruising at 14,000 feet in a good position to intercept the Gothas. Approaching Margate at 10.26 a.m., he observed the 'Readiness' signal from the ground and spotted the formation of Gothas almost straightaway, with the highest flying at 12,000 feet. Later reports say that Brandon did not hesitate but attacked the nearest enemy aircraft, pouring hundreds of rounds into the Gotha and badly damaging its starboard engine. The damage caused the machine to catch fire and it plunged to the ground on Vincent Farm, adjacent to the airfield, just off the Margate road. Its twenty-two-year-old pilot Heinrich Schildt, observer Eckhard Fulda and gunner Ernst Eikelkamp of 15/16 Staffel were killed instantly. The other members of the Gotha's crew who were killed were the twenty-eight-year-old pilot Werner Joschkowitz, and twenty-four-year-old Walter Latowsky. Surprisingly enough, one member of the crew survived – Bruno Schneider was taken as a prisoner of war.

The German crew were buried five days later in St John's Cemetery, Margate, with full military honours but under strange circumstances, the ceremony taking place in the early morning light of dawn. Feelings were running high and there was a lot of tension in the air from the civilian population who were very angry after recent attacks. There was genuine fear that if the service had been carried out in broad daylight there would at least have been demonstrations and possibly attempts to stop the interments. Wing Commander Ross attended the ceremony and, with a large number of ratings and officers marching behind the burial party, the service went as planned.

Brandon's aircraft had not escaped being damaged in the action of 22 August. After being hit by return enemy fire, he had been forced to land back at Manston and take off again in another Camel. His second machine was B3923, named *The Springbok*. The machine had been delivered to the Manston War Flight only ten days earlier, and during its action with Brandon it was also damaged by enemy fire as he pressed home his attack on the Gotha bombers.

As with Scott and Butler on 7 July, several other pilots were involved in the action and there was consequently some confusion about who had shot down what, concerning the Gotha that Brandon claimed and another one that had been destroyed and fallen into the sea off the coast of Margate. The question was whether Brandon's actions had been responsible for shooting down the Gotha, or had it been a victim of the AA guns? Or could it have been another pilot from the War Flight that shot it down?

Not everyone accepted Brandon's version of events. There were further claims that the Gotha had been shot down by two RNAS pilots operating out of Dover, but they were never substantiated. Despite the controversy, many years later, in 1985, two fragments of the Gotha that had survived were presented to the Station Commander. Both were marked with Brandon's name and the date, 22 August 1917. That at least suggests that whoever was responsible for identifying them had officially accepted that it was Brandon who had shot it down.

Squadron Commander Butler is said to have attacked three different Gothas during this action, while Flight Sub-Lieutenant Fitzherbert attacked another one near Ramsgate, and Flight Sub-Lieutenant Harker chased a third machine near Dover. Flight Sub-Lieutenant E. B. Drake attacked a Gotha that was flying near Canterbury and heading for the coast near Dover at 15,500 feet. It is claimed that he chose his victim very carefully and, while making several passes, raked it with his guns as the Gotha finally succumbed to the onslaught and crashed into the sea.

A pilot who was later to become an ace passed through Manston in September when nineteen-year-old Flight Sub-Lieutenant Lionel Ashfield was posted in from Freiston in Lincolnshire. Ashfield, from Wootton Bassett in Wiltshire, had joined the RFC on 29 April 1917 and began his flying training at Eastchurch before being posted to Freiston. He remained with Manston's War Flight until November, when he was posted to No. 2 Squadron at Dunkirk, which later became No. 202 Squadron, on which he was credited with seven enemy aircraft destroyed.

On 26 October 1917, there was a tragic accident at Manston when Flight Lieutenant Brandon was killed. While flying Sopwith Triplane N5382, he collided with a Sopwith Pup, N6466, flown by Lieutenant D. W. Gray. Brandon's death and some details of the incident were reported in *The Times* newspaper on the 29th. After instructing during the afternoon, he had taken off after tea to test the engine of the Triplane, but when he was at about 500 feet the right wing of his aircraft was struck by the Pup, which was descending to land. Brandon had been at Manston less than three months, but he was posthumously awarded the DSC on 17 November. He had flown his last patrol on the 19th in pursuit of Zeppelin L53, which escaped from his attack unscathed.

Brandon's funeral procession began at Hill House Hospital at the top of the village near Tothill Street, not far from Minster Cemetery, and slowly made its way down to the village church. After the service the procession, led by a number of Air Force officers and personnel from Manston, made its way back up the hill to the cemetery for the interment.

A detailed account of the funeral provided by Peter Oliver stated that the village of Minster had never seen such an impressive ceremony as the funeral

Right: It is understood that this photo shows the wreckage of Flight Lieutenant Brandon's Sopwith Triplane, N5382, on the airfield at Manston. This can not be confirmed but the gloomy faces seem to indicate that they have just witnessed a tragic event. The aircraft does not appear to be badly damaged but it looks like it was inverted when it hit the ground and that the tail has been lifted, probably to remove Flight Lieutenant Brandon's body. (*Peter Oliver*)

Below: The Funeral Procession for Flight Lieutenant Brandon held in Minster on what appears to be a very wet day. His coffin was carried on a gun carriage and draped with the Union Jack. (*Peter Oliver*)

Above: Flight Lieutenant Brandon's grave covered with a huge mound of flowers in Minster Cemetery. A crowd of sombre looking servicemen from Manston are in the background and on the extreme right there appears to be two women, one of whom may have been Brandon's sister. (*Peter Oliver*)

Left: Flight Lieutenant Brandon's grave and headstone in Minster Cemetery with his medal – the DSC – now owned by local historian Peter Oliver. (*Peter Oliver*)

held on that Tuesday afternoon. Crowds of people lined the main street as the coffin was borne to the parish church on a gun carriage, the six horses being driven by three fellow officers. The cortege was met at the gates of the churchyard gates by the vicar, Canon A. E. Molineux, who was accompanied by the Chaplin from RNAS Manston.

> The coffin, draped in the Union Jack, was placed upon a bier and borne into the church by eight of the deceased fellow officers, with the large contingent of officers and men of the RNAS standing at the salute. There was the chanting of prayers as the coffin made its way up the path and in the church a short service was conducted by the vicar who was assisted by the chaplain. With the service concluded the coffin was again placed upon the gun carriage and the procession formed up. Heading the process were the men of the RNAS who were followed by the band of the Northumberland Fusilers, with its drums muffled.

A headstone was later placed on the grave, but it is not clear who paid for it, as it is understood that his only living relative was a sister who lived in South Africa. It was noted on the base of the headstone that Brandon had also served throughout the German South West African Campaign and in Salonika, and that he was the third son of the late Charles Brandon of Montreal and Mrs D. R. Conradie of Harrismith, South Africa. On top of the grave a plaque was placed in memory of Brandon's cousin, twenty-two-year-old Lieutenant Edgar Thomas Colin Brandon, who had been killed while flying on operations over Arras on 3 April 1917. His body was never recovered, and he is also commemorated on the Arras Flying Services Memorial.

The inscription on the base of the headstone reads:

> Both so joyous in life and duty
> And most deeply regretted
> Their duty nobly done.

Ironically, three days later, one of the Camels that Brandon had flown in action on 22 August, B3923 *The Springbok*, was scrapped. It had been damaged in the action that day and after being surveyed it was decided that it was not worth repairing. The other Camel that Brandon had flown that day, B3834 *Wonga Bonga*, was not struck off charge until February 1918.

Various works and additions of buildings were authorised on 20 September, with the approval for the erection of a permanent building or shed to accommodate the Handley Page bombers. A few weeks later, work began on the building of large workshops suitable for carrying out repairs to the Handley Page aeroplane. Although it cannot be confirmed, this is probably the authorisation to build what were later known as the underground hangars. As the airfield expanded, the Station Headquarters building was the first to be completed in 1917, but many others would soon be built around it.

In September 1917, 'A' Squadron was formed out of No. 7A Squadron at Manston with a number of Handley Page bombers that had arrived at Manston from various different units. Four of them came from a detachment of No. 7 Squadron at Redcar, four from Hendon, and two from the main base of No. 7 Squadron at Coudekerque in France. During four weeks of coastal patrol operations at Redcar, the aircraft had sighted eleven enemy submarines and bombed seven of them, but none were confirmed as being sunk. At Manston the HP O/100s also carried out regular coastal patrols of the North Sea while they waited for orders to be moved to France. By August 1917, Squadrons 7 & 7A had a total of twenty HP O/100s available to them.

Although 'A' Squadron was documented as a separate unit, it was still part of and controlled by No. 7 Squadron. According to its official history, 'A' Squadron was never officially based at Manston but used it as a forward airfield from where aeroplanes were delivered to France, and also for supporting and training its pilots and other crews converting to the HP O/100.

On the last day of September, a Gotha attacked Margate, dropping its bombs on Cliff Terrace and killing three Sappers from the Royal Engineers Waterways and Docks Section who had just returned from leave. They were based at the port of Richborough, but had missed their train and were in the process of walking to report to the local military HQ in Dalby Square. The bodies of Sappers J. McGratty, F. Williams and T. Armstrong were so badly mangled that they were buried in a common grave in Margate Cemetery.

There were a number of awards made to airmen and officers at Manston and Westgate in October. Flight Sub-Lieutenants Carr, de Sallis and Morris received the DSC for their contribution to patrol duties and searching for submarines in home waters. Even the air mechanics were honoured, six of them receiving the DSM. They were Air Mechanics D. A. Alderton, H. M. Lewis, H. D. Gregory, A. K. Wise, G. L. Wight, and W. E. Bradley. Flight Sub-Lieutenant Mills had previously been mentioned in despatches.

To keep 'A' Squadron up to strength it was re-equipped with more HP O/100s to replace the Short Bombers. The squadron handed over a number of Shorts for disposal at Manston, and the type had been taken out of service in April 1917. The Short Bomber had entered service with No. 7 Squadron RNAS and flown its first operation on the night of 15 November 1916 against objectives at Ostend.

The advance party of 'A' Squadron left Manston on 4 October for Hautvillers in France and became part of the 41st Wing GHQ Brigade. On the 10th, the first four HP O/100s left Manston for Dunkirk *en route* to Ochey. The Manston Diary rather unusually gave the nature of their operations and

This tragic scene is believed to be Handley Page O/100, serial number 3116, which crashed on 3 November 1917 killing three of the crew. (*Chris Lofft*)

objectives, stating that they were to be used for bombing operations against German munitions centres in co-operation with the RFC.

While converting to the HP O/100 there were a number of accidents, and on 3 November 1917 an aeroplane from 'A' Squadron, 3116, crashed killing three of its crew and seriously injuring another three. The machine had already served in France and had been the first one to land at Coudekerque after a raid on Thorout railway station on 15 July. Twenty-one-year-old Flight Sub-Lieutenant Joseph A. St James, twenty-two-year-old Flight Sub-Lieutenant Walter Albert Isaacs from Leytonstone, and twenty-year-old Probationary Flight Officer Thomas Reginald Weston of Kensal Green were those members of the crew killed. Only St James, who came from Saint-Constant, Quebec, Canada, was buried locally in Minster Cemetery, while Isaacs was buried at Woodgrange Park Cemetery in Essex, and Weston at Pinner Cemetery in Middlesex.

Because of the number of hostile air raids in the area around Manston, on all nights when there was a bright moon a single aeroplane was provided for observation work. The pilot was not only to keep a look-out for enemy machines but also to observe the weather conditions and in particular the visibility, details of which were then to be sent to the C-in-C of the Nore Command.

Although the main aerial activity was taking place at Manston, it should not be forgotten that the Royal Naval Station at Westgate was still operational with its seaplanes. In November 1917, Squadron Commander Ross was posted out and Squadron Commander Eustace de Courcy Hallifax took over his command.

The RNAS station at Westgate suffered another casualty on 6 November when Flight Sub-Lieutenant George Hodges Herriot was killed while flying in a Fairey Hamble Baby, N1327, reportedly having fallen out of the aeroplane. It was a single-seat wooden-structured machine covered with fabric and powered by a 110 hp Clerget engine that was normally used on anti-submarine patrols.

Herriot was twenty years old and although he had been born in Glasgow, his family had moved on a number of occasions because of his father's profession. When he was only three years of age, in 1899, his family had moved to the USA, sailing from Liverpool to Boston on board the SS *Derbyshire*, but by 1901 they had returned and were living in Birchtree Road, Widnes. In the 1911 census, Herriot's father John was listed as a marine surveyor working for the Board of Trade in Belfast and was forty-four years old. Both George Herriot and his older brother Thomas were subsequently educated at Campbell College in

The grave of twenty-year-old Flight Sub-Lieutenant G. H. Herriot, who was killed while flying off the coast near Westgate on 6 November 1917. (*Joe Bamford*)

Belfast and, in 1914, Thomas also joined the RNAS after gaining his degree at Queen's University, Belfast. On 4 June 1917, Thomas had been awarded his Royal Aero Club Certificate, No. 4797, and followed his younger brother into a career in naval aviation. Thomas also completed the proud family tradition of a father with two sons following him into Royal Navy service.

George Hodges Herriot was buried in Minster Cemetery, and twenty-six years later, his seventy-five-year-old father, Engineer Commander John Scott Herriot, was buried in the same grave. Former Commander Herriot died of natural causes on 22 February 1943. Thomas later graduated from Cranwell and was recommended to serve on seaplanes, training at Lee-on-Solent and Calshot. In November 1918, he was listed as a Lieutenant in the RAF. Thomas was commissioned again in 1939 as a Flying Officer and survived the Second World War to relinquish his commission finally in July 1954 with the rank of Flight Lieutenant, having been awarded the DSC and MBE.

In early December, it was decided that the Manston War Flight should be run down and that its machines should only patrol an area from Manston to Ramsgate, and then another area across to the North Foreland and back to Manston. Orders were issued stating that aeroplanes in Nore Command were no longer to be used to defend the local area from attack by enemy aeroplanes. In their newly designated role, its aeroplanes were to be used solely for instructional purposes, but it would continue to be responsible for shipping patrols. The establishment of the War Flight was reduced to just four pilots – a far cry from the heady days of August when its pilots had destroyed a number of Gotha bombers.

The command of Manston's parent station at Westgate changed again in November, and Hallifax, who had taken over from Squadron Commander Ross, was replaced by Major-General Edward Livock. Ross and Livock were good friends, having served together as pilots on HMS *Engadine* in 1914. Livock, who came from Newmarket had joined the RNAS straight from school, had gained his Royal Aero Club Certificate, No. 1004, on 20 December 1914. He had learned to fly at RNAS Hendon where his instructor was, unusually, a Russian, but what he learned from him would come in handy in future years.

In December 1917, questions were asked in Parliament about the land titled Manston Park that had been requisitioned as part of the airfield at Manston. Manston Park is situated to the north-east of the airfield and is currently occupied by a business centre. Sir Herbert Nield requested that the Personal Secretary of the Admiralty should state whether it had been under the Statutory Enactment Regulations or under other regulations that the land at Manston Park near Margate had been possessed. The land was owned by a Mr J. Proctor, and he wanted to know if it had been proposed that the Government should occupy the land permanently and, if so, what were the reasons for delaying negotiations for its purchase.

The reply was given by no less a person than Winston Churchill, who said that the land had been occupied under the Defence of the Realm Act and that the decision about RNAS Manston's future had only recently been made. It had now been decided that the airfield should be a permanent station, and the Air Ministry intended to retain the land. In its opinion, the owner had not suffered any loss, and the matter would be discussed further when the Air Ministry was in a position to take further action. This was the first time that the future of Manston had been mentioned and, in the short term at least, its future was secured, but it had already been mooted that one of its largest units would shortly have to move out.

During the night of 22–23 December, another unexpected visitor arrived over Thanet in the form of a Gotha bomber from Bogohl III that was based near Ghent. The aircraft was brought down not because of any action by Allied aircraft or AA guns but because of engine failure, and it crash landed in Margate behind what is now Hartsdown Secondary School. The Gotha may well have landed intact, but the actions of the pilot, Unteroffizier Hoffman, and his crew ensured that it did not fall into British hands. A flare was fired into the machine and the Gotha was set on fire and totally burned out, and the only satisfaction that the authorities had was that all three airmen were taken as prisoners of war.

On 23 December, a letter was sent to the Commanding Officer at Manston from the Director of Air Services, based in the Hotel Cecil on the Strand in London. It contained details about the proposed move of the Handley Page Training Flight from Manston to Stonehenge and gave a situation report as the unit was at Manston. The list of personnel of the Handley Page unit named Squadron Commander Thomson as the Officer Commanding, with the two instructors for the Handley Page machines being Flight Lieutenant Souray and Flight Sub-Lieutenant Waterton. Squadron Commander Stanley Adams had joined the unit on a temporary basis, his main role being to give lectures on navigation.

The same document stating that Thomson was to command the Handley Page unit at Stonehenge expressed considerable doubts about whether he was experienced enough to carry it out. It was pointed out that both the RFC's Commanding Officer at Stonehenge, as well as several RFC instructors, had taken part in raids on enemy positions. Neither Thomson, Souray nor Waterton had had the benefit of that experience. It was stated that the officer in charge of the unit should be selected from those who had flown Handley Pages under active service conditions. It appears that there were a lot of 'double dealings' going on.

The instructors for the DH.4 at Stonehenge were named as Flight Commander Gardner and Flight Lieutenants Ovens, Shore, and Sawnston. The Engineering Officer was Lieutenant Young, the Armament Officer was

Lieutenant Ashworth, and the Observer/WT Officer was Lieutenant Thomson. It must have been quite confusing, because apart from the latter and CO being named Thomson, there was also a Stores Officer called Warrant Officer Thomson.

The Handley Page Training Flight had between sixty and seventy pupils on its strength, with their instruction being divided equally between the Handley Page machines and the DH.4. There were two HP O/100s being used for training and another two belonging to Dunkirk that were being reconstructed. It was reported that one of them, 1465, had been test flown on 23 December and declared ready for use. The Flight also had eleven DH.4s for initial pilot training, but four of them were without engines and awaiting rebuilds. Pilots averaged between ten and twelve hours a month flying on the DH.4, but with the arrival of more machines it was estimated that would increase to between 60 and 70 hours of training.

There was a permanent complement of 330 ratings on the Handley Page Flight, but 124 of those were destined to be posted to the new squadrons which were being formed. It was also noted that the Flight was not only responsible for the formation of squadrons with Handley Page aeroplanes but also the reconstruction of the machines based at Dunkirk. In a document written on 23 December, it was stated that the unit was also responsible for training the Handley Page pilots. The comments seemed to be made in such a way as to suggest that someone in command did not appreciate the role carried out by the Flight or agree with the move!

CHAPTER 6

1918: RAF Manston

In January 1918, the Admiralty together with the War Office decided that in future the RFC would be responsible for the Nore area against hostile enemy action, and instructions were issued that Manston was to be regarded mainly as an instructional unit. Orders were also given that the aeroplanes of the War Flight were to be put at the disposal of No. 50 (HD) Squadron, based at Dover. It was decided that Manston would still remain as one of two naval air stations responsible for the defence of merchant shipping and the maintenance of anti-submarine patrols.

Squadron Commander Butler, who had commanded the War Flight at both Westgate and Manston, was posted to Dunkirk in January. His valuable experience was badly missed at Manston, and within a few months he would take over command of No. 9 (RNAS) Squadron, passing his skill and knowledge on to a younger generation.

There were a number of movements in and out of Manston in early 1918, but one of the most significant was that of the Handley Page Training Flight with its HP O/100 bombers, which moved out to Stonehenge in Wiltshire. Although not one of the most renowned airfields, Stonehenge had its place in aviation history as it was the scene of the first ever fatal crash of an aeroplane from the RFC. The incident had occurred on 5 July 1912, when Captain Loraine and his observer, Staff Sergeant Wilson, were both killed.

From what has been documented in the official records it is quite clear that there was some disagreement about who should become the Commanding Officer of the unit after its move to Stonehenge. It was intimated that Squadron Commander Thomson, who was currently in command of the Handley Page Training Flight, did not have the necessary skills to command the Flight at Stonehenge. That was because he lacked active service experience on Handley Page aircraft, and it was considered desirable that whoever commanded the unit should be up to date with the method of employment of the machines under active service conditions.

Thomson's main duties at Manston had been the formation, fitting up and collecting of stores for those squadrons that were about to proceed to France. Another argument that went against him being appointed to command the unit at Stonehenge was that the valuable experience he had in those areas would be lost if he was posted away. It was therefore considered desirable that he should remain at Manston. That would have been possible because it had been proposed that not all of the Handley Page Training Flight should move out and that the formation and fitting out of the squadrons, as well as the training and fitting out on the DH.4s, should remain at Manston. However, the authorities decided against that, and the whole unit moved to Stonehenge. It was suggested that 200 ratings should be left at Manston for the DH.4 training and the fitting out of the aeroplanes. On the original document containing these proposals, someone had written the word 'no' to all those points.

Despite the fact that Thomson's role as the Commanding Officer of the Handley Page Training Flight at Stonehenge had been questioned, his appointment was confirmed in a letter from the Director of Air Services dated 8 January. It was headed 'Air Department Acquaint No. 57: Transfer of Handley Page Training Flight from Manston to Stonehenge' and clearly stated, 'Squadron Commander Thomson will be appointed in charge of the RNAS station at Stonehenge and every facility.'

Six machines were allocated to Stonehenge, and the total personnel posted there comprised 60 officers and 250 ratings. The part of the school that used the DH.4s for initial pilot training was to remain at Manston. On completion of their training they would be posted to Stonehenge. It was noted that the stores at Manston were to send their demands for bedding and 'messtraps' as soon as possible, but ratings were ordered to take their bedding and hammocks with them anyway. Despite being an air service, naval traditions and the use of hammocks had to be maintained at all costs!

The airfield at Stonehenge was just a short distance from the world-famous historic henge monument, approximately two-and-a-half miles west of Amesbury just off what is today the A303. One can only imagine the outcry if for any reason the historic monument had been damaged or destroyed by an aircraft crashing or having to make a forced landing. The accommodation for RAF personnel was, however, one-and-a-half miles from the airfield and they had to rely on civilian transport to get them there. There was no lighting in the hangars, and there were urgent, last-minute preparations for the squadron to be accommodated and organised.

There remains some confusion about the role of Babington as Manston's Commanding Officer. According to a number of documents and different sources, he had taken over command of Manston in May 1917. Having handed over the command of No. 7 Squadron to a former member of the Manston War Flight, Squadron Commander H. A. Buss, he had returned to England in the New Year. Some accounts of his personal record state that he remained in that post until September 1918, while also stating that he was the Officer Commanding the Handley Page Training Flight that had recently moved to Stonehenge. The two stations being a considerable distance apart, it is difficult to understand how he could have functioned in both roles. It is much more likely that the command of Manston was passed to Wing Commander Smyth-Osbourne, who had formerly been the Officer in Command of the Nore under its Commander-in-Chief. Various biographies of Smyth-Osbourne claim that he was the Commanding Officer of Manston until April 1918, but there is nothing in the records to confirm that appointment.

The move to Stonehenge was to end Babington's connections with Manston and Westgate that had lasted nearly three years. But he still had a long and illustrious service career ahead of him. In August 1919, he was awarded a permanent commission, and the following year was removed from the Navy List to that of the RAF. He later became the AOC of both 24 Group and the Technical Training Group, remaining in the service until he retired in February 1944. Strangely enough, John Tremayne Babington's younger brother Philip, who was commissioned into the Army in 1914, also learned to fly, transferred to the RAF and also reached air rank to become the AOC of Flying Training Command.

When the Commanding Officer of the War Flight, Squadron Commander Butler, was posted out of Manston on 31 January 1918, it spelt the end of the unit, if the reduction in the number of pilots had not already done so. He had been at Westgate and then Manston for two and a half years and under his leadership the War Flight had flourished. He was posted to Dunkirk to command No. 209 Squadron – the unit most associated with the death of German ace Manfred von Richthofen.

There were a number of fatal accidents at Manston in February, the first one on the 12th involving 2nd Lieutenant Donald Roy Glenn of the War Flight whose Camel, B6554, spun into the ground from 500 feet. Glenn, who was a Canadian from Indian Head, Saskatchewan, was buried in Minster Cemetery and, according to information held by the Commonwealth War Graves Commission and other sources, was just seventeen years old.

If February was a bad month, March was not much better. On the 6th, Flight Sub-Lieutenant Wilfred Norman Cross of the War School was killed while flying Sopwith Camel B5734. The eighteen-year-old pilot, a native of St Leonards-on-Sea, was buried in Minster Cemetery. The War School lost another of its young pilots on the 10th when nineteen-year-old 2nd Lieutenant John William Kavanagh crashed into the sea just off the coast of Ramsgate while flying in Camel N6343. Although he was reported missing when he failed to return to Manston, his aeroplane and body were not found until the next day. Kavanagh, who was a member of the RFC and was from Claremont, Cape Province, in South Africa, was buried in Ramsgate Cemetery.

Rather unusually, Kavanagh's death was reported in some detail by the local newspaper under the headline 'Fatality In Fog: Sad Fate of Young Flying Officer'. The article focused on the subsequent inquest conducted by Dr F. W. Hardman and a jury made up of seven members of the public. It was stated that Kavanagh had taken off from Manston during the late afternoon on Sunday in a slight ground mist that had quickly turned into fog. In the opinion of a witness, Flight Lieutenant MacFarlane, the conditions were such that Kavanagh would have been unable to distinguish between the sea and land. The aeroplane was only found by accident when a vessel that had been moored in Ramsgate Harbour overnight fetched up its anchor and raised the Camel from the seabed with Kavanagh's body still strapped inside it.

One of the main criticisms of a member of the jury was that the wreck of the aeroplane had been removed from the scene and the jury were not allowed to inspect it, although what the jury or Coroner would have gained by seeing the wreck we will never know. The Coroner quoted the Defence of the Realm Act, but that particular member of the jury said that the Act was a farce and asked him why the authorities did not arrest the 'Germans'. That comment probably echoed the sentiment of a large part of the community, in which fear of the Germans, and especially spies, was commonplace.

After Kavanagh's body had been removed from the aeroplane it was taken to the mortuary and was examined by Dr Stvan who found that external injuries included abrasions to both knees and a cut on the lower lip three inches long, and that one tooth was missing. He also had an injury to his head that was consistent with him having hit his head on the machine gun, and it was considered quite probable that the blow had knocked him unconscious. The Coroner and jury therefore came to the view that Kavanagh had died from drowning. Members of the jury asked MacFarlane to convey their sympathy to his family.

On 30 March, twenty-two-year-old Flight Sub-Lieutenant Norman Mallard spun into the sea off Westgate while flying Camel B3832, which had been delivered to Manston from Dover on 18 February. He was buried in his home town of Ilkey in Yorkshire.

One of the student pilots who passed through Manston's War School at this time was aviation pioneer and stunt pilot Alan Cobham, who had just re-mustered to the RFC. He was at the time known as an 'Old Contemptible' – a veteran of the British Expeditionary Force – and had returned to England after spending three and half years in France. After re-mustering to the RFC, he spent six weeks in the recruiting centre at Denham before being sent to Manston for flying training.

During his time at Manston, and despite being a member of the RFC and a student of the RNAS Flying School, Cobham continued to wear his Army khaki uniform. It is claimed that he did not give that up until he was commissioned.

He then went on to gain experience of a number of types such as the B.E.2c and the B.E.2e, and was regularly accompanied into the air by Captain Keble. Cobham must have been a good pilot, because after only 40 hours' instruction he was made an instructor on No. 55 Training Depot Station and was posted to Manston when No. 55 TDS moved there later in the year, continuing as an instructor with the unit after it moved from Manston.

With the building of new hangars and other facilities, after the departure of the Handley Page Training Flight there was plenty of room at Manston, with extensions to buildings that had been authorised the previous August. There was accommodation for 270 officers and 3,355 airmen lying empty, so at the beginning of April it was decided that No. 203 TDS should move in. Its arrival gave further clues to the fact that Manston's new role was to be as a training station rather than as an operational one. No. 203 TDS was made up with the equivalent of three day bomber squadrons initially equipped with the BE.2e, two examples of which on its strength were B4575 and B4586.

On 1 April 1918, the Royal Naval Air Service merged with the Royal Flying Corps to form the Royal Air Force. It was not a move favoured by many of those in the RNAS who thought that they had come out of it as 'second best'. There were a number of reasons for that, but it was a fact that RNAS squadrons had to add 200 to their unit number (No. 7 Squadron RNAS became No. 207 Squadron, No. 16 Squadron RNAS became 216 Squadron, etc.) and Navy personnel with precious low numbers from the earliest days of the service were obliged to add a number of zeros to their service number, which suggested that they had only recently joined up.

There would undoubtedly have been mixed feeling as the flag of the RNAS was lowered at Manston for the last time on the evening of 31 March and the flag of the RAF was raised for the first time. However, on most stations there was already a mixture of personnel from the RFC and the RNAS, some of whom came from Australia, Canada and South Africa, and they would have had mixed loyalties anyway. It was not just flags and ensigns that were different, but custom, dress and rank were all adjusted over a period of time.

The RAF took some titles for the ranks of its officers from the Army, and those in command of a Wing were typically Lieutenant-Colonels, but it was decided to use some of the Royal Navy's terms such as 'Commander' and hence they became known as Wing Commanders. In the RFC an officer with the rank of major had normally commanded a squadron and it was decided to change that to 'Air Lieutenant Commander'. The Navy had used the term 'Squadron Commander' and objected to the corruption of the title, so it was decided to use the title Squadron Leader. On the issue of titles for RAF officers, the Navy may have come off best and some of its heritage was saved.

The strength of RAF Manston on 1 April 1918 was 139 officers, 973 airmen, and 111 aeroplanes. It was broken down by unit as follows:

	Officers	Airmen	Aeroplanes
203 Training Depot Station	51	554	54
Pilot Pool	62	303	39
470 War Flight	6	36	6
555 Flight	10	40	6
556 Flight	10	40	6
Totals	139	973	111

Strangely enough, the War Flight was acknowledged as being part of No. 219 Squadron, but that unit would not be formed for another three months. There could be a simple explanation for that, if the Manston Diary was written up after the forming of No. 219 Squadron. The establishment of aeroplanes between all the units was given as DH.4s, SE.5s, Dolphins, Bristol Fighters, Camels, Avros, and SPADs.

The RAF was still actively recruiting, and a poster advertising vacancies in the service invited applicants to 'Join the Royal Air Force and Share their Honour and Glory'. It was accepting applicants aged between eighteen and fifty years, and rates of pay ranged from 1s 6d to 12s a day. From 1 April, women were allowed into the Air Force with the launch of the Women's Royal Air Force. They were wanted as clerks, waitresses, cooks and motorcyclists, and were encouraged to get further information from their local employment exchange.

After the formation of the RAF, former RNAS and RAF stations became known as Air Contingents and stations were divided up into groups. Westgate, along with other RNAS stations at Felixstowe and Yarmouth, became part of No. 4 Group under the control of Commander Charles Rumney Samson. Since 1912, when he had commanded the Naval Flying School at Eastchurch, Samson had served overseas with No. 3 Squadron (later No. 3 Wing) and had been involved in the action at Gallipoli, commanding a unit based on the island of Tenedos and a number of seaplanes from HMS *Ark Royal*. Initially they had provided the only air cover, and Samson pioneered the use of radio to guide the guns of the ships to their targets on the shore.

As part of the organisational changes after the merger of the RNAS and the RFC, or in some cases before the merger, the names of a number of units were changed. At Manston the War School became the Pilots' Pool, and among the aircraft it had on its strength were a number of Sopwith Camels, including B6204, B6217, B6291, B6225, and B6230. A number of those had quite chequered histories; B6217, which had been delivered into service with 9N Squadron, had shared in the destruction of a number of Albatrosses in September 1917, before arriving at Manston via Dover; B6225 had seen service with 10N Squadron and been damaged by gunfire on 25 September, but also later shared in the destruction of an enemy aeroplane.

One thing that did not change with the formation of the RAF was the accident rate, and the first serious incident at Manston after the merger occurred on 6 April and involved eighteen-year-old 2nd Lieutenant Howard Raymond Gillett. The only son of Mr and Mrs Raymond Gillett, he was killed while he was flying Sopwith Camel B6588 that had been delivered to Manston in November 1917 and entered service with the War School on the 24th. Gillett was buried in Hampstead, London.

There are some details of another incident on 21 April, with mention of an incident or crash on that date, and two days later, Air Mechanic 1st Class Bertie Reynolds (213766) was killed, but there is no information about how he died. Reynolds was buried in St George's Cemetery, Handsworth.

There were a number of changes in the structure of the units at both Westgate and Manston in May, and on the 25th of that month 406 Seaplane Flight was formed at Westgate. It was equipped with a Sopwith 184, the single-seat tractor-powered Sopwith Baby and the Fairey Hamble, otherwise known as the Admiralty type 8200 Baby. At Manston on 27 May 1918, 470 (Fighter) Flight was formed out of an amalgamation of the War Flight and was equipped with six Sopwith Camels. The unit was also known as the Tongue Defence Flight, the name referring to its main area of operations around the Tongue light vessel.

There was an unconfirmed reported that one of 470 Flight's Camels had experienced a close encounter with an enemy submarine on 31 May, and though few details of the incident survive, it is known that the aircraft involved was N6634. The machine had previously served with the RNAS at Yarmouth and its last noted movement was when it had been sent to Felixstowe. Details of the pilot involved and whether the U-boat was damaged or sunk were not recorded.

Two more deaths occurred on 2 July when a B.E.2c, 9989, crashed to the ground after it stalled while in a steep turn and its pilot was unable to recover the aeroplane. Two airmen were killed: twenty-five-year-old Flight Sergeant William Rowland Felton from Ilford, and 2nd Lieutenant Edward Percival John Hull from London. Felton was buried in his native town of Ilford, while Hull was buried in Abney Park Cemetery, London. There is a report claiming that the accident happened after a collision between Felton's B.E.2c and Hull's SPAD S.7, A8834, but there are other conflicting reports about the exact details of the incident.

On 4 July, a patrol from Westgate – a flight of seaplanes led by Major Livock – attempted to intercept four Brandenburg W.29 seaplanes that had attacked and badly damaged three Curtiss flying boats from Felixstowe. The German seaplanes, on their very first mission, were fitted with a powerful 150 hp Benz engine and armed with two forward firing machine guns and one rear firing gun for the use of the observer. The W.29 was a monoplane built to replace the

Brandenburg W.12 biplane. It had first flown on 27 March and had a top speed of 109 mph. Fast enough to outrun most British seaplanes and some biplanes, but particularly those slow flying boats that operated out of Felixstowe, it was used mainly to attack fast surface vessels such as motor launches, but was also capable of being used in aerial combat. Livock's patrol failed to find any W.29s and subsequently encountered nothing more threatening that an oil slick close to the Tongue light ship.

Number 55 TDS moved into Manston on 14 July and, like No. 203 TDS, it was soon re-equipped with the DH.9. However, the type did not have the best of reputations, having suffered heavy losses with the RAF over the Western Front. The DH.9A, fitted with the 400 hp Liberty L-12 engine, was an improvement, but it was still unable to match the performance of other British aircraft such as the Camel.

On 17 July, there was a very bad collision between two Sopwith Pups from the recently formed Pilots' Pool involving Sergeant Edward Harper Sayers flying in B5992, and Sergeant John Dudley Bishop in 9901. The aeroplanes collided just outside the airfield boundary and both pilots were killed instantly. Twenty-year-old Sayers (12315), born at Merton in Surrey, was

The grave of Sergeant John Dudley Bishop who was killed in a flying accident at the tender age of eighteen on 17 July 1918, with a view across the cemetery at Minster. (*Joe Bamford*)

buried at Ealing in Middlesex. Originally serving as an air mechanic, Sayers had already escaped death on a number of occasions. On 14 April 1917, while serving on No. 20 Squadron and flying with Lieutenant Perry, he had been shot down over Polygon Wood. On 30 April 1917, while flying with Lieutenant Hay, his aeroplane had been hit by AA fire and crashed, with both men being injured. His aeroplane was hit and damaged again on 8 June, but 2nd Lieutenant Durrand got them back safely. He was notified on 31 May that he had been awarded the French Médaille Militaire and on his return to the Home Establishment had trained as a pilot. After all he had gone through, it was truly ironic that he should be killed in such a tragic accident.

The Commonwealth War Graves Commission holds very little information about Sergeant Bishop (100069) with the exception of his service number and the fact that he is buried in Minster Cemetery. However, it is obvious from the inscription on the headstone of his grave that he had a family that missed him very much. It says simply, 'The irreparable loss of a much loved son'.

Two more Flights, Nos 555 and 556, were soon added to the War Flight and, along with No. 470 Squadron at Westgate, they were all absorbed into No. 219 Squadron when it was formed on 22 July. There had not been a No. 219 Squadron before, and effectively it was the first unit (squadron) as such to be formed at Manston. Its main role was to escort the seaplanes from Westgate, but as we shall soon discover, it was not always very successful. The Commanding Officer of No. 219 Squadron was Major G. E. Livock, thus keeping the connection between Manston and Westgate alive.

Exactly two weeks after the new German Brandenburg seaplane had made its first appearance attacking a number of flying boats from Felixstowe, another incident occurred that proved their superiority over British aeroplanes, but seaplanes in particular. On 18 July, two Short seaplanes from Westgate – N2927, Lieutenant Joseph Albert Edward Vowles with observer Lieutenant James Garney Marshall Farrall, and N2937, Lieutenants Jack Arthur Horton Pegram and Leonard Albert Thrower – were sent out to patrol the area around the Kentish Knock. As was the operational procedure at that time, the seaplanes from Westgate were accompanied by two Sopwith Camels from Manston: on this occasion, B5601 with Lieutenant F. C. Vincent, and Lieutenant Wagstaff in B7628. Five miles east of the Kentish Knock the British seaplanes were attacked by a pack of five Brandenburg seaplanes of the German Flanders 1 unit and an enemy biplane that dived on them out of the sun. It took them totally by surprise and the pilots of the two Camels were unable to intervene until it was too late.

The Short seaplane N2927 was the fist victim. It crashed into the sea, smashing its floats on the water and catching fire soon afterwards. There was nothing that either Vincent or Wagstaff could do, but the two Camels mingled with the German aeroplanes as best they could. However, they were outnumbered and unable to prevent the other Short seaplane being attacked. Before long, the second Short seaplane crashed into the sea and there was a lot of confusion among the two Camel pilots about what they had witnessed. The two pilots from Manston were convinced that what they had seen was the German biplane being shot down. When they landed back at Manston, they reported that one of the seaplanes had survived the engagement and was on its way back to Westgate. One of the two Camel pilots was even convinced that he had destroyed a Brandenburg seaplane, but that proved not to be the case either and the Germans had even taken photographs of the action to prove their case.

When neither of the Short seaplanes failed to arrive back at Westgate, Lieutenants Landar and Shaw were dispatched to carry out a search, but by then it was blowing a gale with a Force 5 wind and a very rough sea. When they flew over the scene of the incident there was no sign of either the seaplanes or their crews, and despite an extensive search, their bodies were never found. In terms of loss of life, this incident on 18 July was the worst to happen involving airmen from Westgate or Manston during the First World War. Lieutenants Vowles, Farrall, Pegram and Thrower are all commemorated on the Hollybrook Memorial in Southampton.

On 24 July, two pilots and a machine were lost from No. 55 TDS, which had formed at Manston on 14 July, when Flight Cadet Thomas Turner Whitley and Air Mechanic 1st Class Alfred Capes were killed while in a DH.9, B7608. Delivered to Manston from Brooklands on 23 February 1918, it had served with both Nos 55 and 203 TDS. This was the first of a number of incidents involving the DH.9, which had entered service with the RFC in November the previous year. Whitley (321403) was eighteen years old and came from Bingley in West Yorkshire, where he was buried. Capes (213323) was thirty-two years old and from Bethnal Green, but was buried in Minster Cemetery.

This accident was witnessed by Lieutenant-Colonel Arthur Borton (Retired) who was taking a leisurely stroll after breakfast along the esplanade at Ramsgate in anticipation of his son arriving at Manston in a Handley Page O/400. His son, Brigadier Amyas Borton, and Major Archibald McLaren were flying from Cranwell in a brand new aeroplane, C9681, and were about to attempt a record-breaking flight to the Middle East.

Lieutenant-Colonel Borton noted in his diary that he saw a DH.9 over the sea, about half-a-mile off the coast, when suddenly it entered a steep dive. The left wing fell away when the aeroplane was approximately 150 feet above the sea, and after hitting the water the DH.9 turned over several times. It was later discovered that there had been a structural failure with the wing and that when the aircraft crashed, the engine had been under full power. Although part of the aeroplane had remained floating on the water, the bodies of the two crewmen had disappeared and were probably carried away by the tide. It was approximately a quarter of an hour before the first boat arrived on the scene and by that time it was far too late for any rescue attempt to be made.

The HP O/400 arrived at Manston the following day. Lieutenant-Colonel Borton described how the aeroplane appeared in the distance before approaching the airfield and making a perfect landing. Among other family to greet the crew at Manston, along with Borton's parents was Major McLaren's wife. After the engines were shut down, the wings of the O/400 were then folded away and it was wheeled into a shed where it remained for the next three days. There it was prepared for the flight to Paris and beyond a few days later.

Having greeted his son and checked that the aeroplane was safely tucked away, Borton and his party returned to their hotel in Ramsgate. After dinner they observed an aeroplane that was flying along the seafront. While making what he described as a bad flat turn, the aeroplane suddenly entered a sharp spiral dive towards the sea and crashed very close to a nearby outcrop of rocks. Fortunately on this occasion the pilot survived and escaped with just some cuts on his face, but for Borton the dangers of flying had been made clear. In just two days at Ramsgate he had witnessed two serious accidents in which two airmen had lost their lives. That could not have been a good omen, with his son about to embark on an epic and perilous journey to the Middle East.

The HP O/400 departed from Manston for France on 28 July, and when Lieutenant-Colonel Borton arrived there at 2.30 p.m. he described the air as being full of machines with some of them looping about the sky. The HP O/400 was sat outside the shed, with its wings fully open, ready for its flight to distant shores, and after the engines were started and run up to full power, at 3.15 p.m. the machine taxied out to the runway. Without further ceremony the aeroplane then turned around and took off. It rose into the air very easily and after it had completed one small circuit, Borton and his party waved their final farewells before it disappeared into the distance and out of sight. There were four airmen on board, and the crew was made up with mechanics Flight Sergeant Goldfinch and Air Mechanic Francis. Eleven days and 2,592 miles later, and having landed at Alexandria to pick up the AOC Middle East, Geoffrey Salmond, the machine touched down at Heliopolis in Egypt. That night, the feat made the headlines in the *Evening Standard*, but it was to make even greater news a short while later. That was during the Battle of Megiddo, when the Handley Page machine was used to bomb the Turkish HQ and telephone exchange in Al-Fuleh. Manston had played a small part in another historical event.

On 29 July, No. 55 TDS suffered a further fatality when another DH.9, D3118, stalled in a turn and spun into the ground from 500 feet. Air Mechanic 2nd Class George Frederick Frost was killed. The twenty-year-old was buried in his home town of Wellington in Shropshire. The pilot, Flight Cadet R. J. Wickam, was lucky to escape with his life, although he was seriously injured. Rather ironically, Wickam had had his photograph taken just a short while before his ill-fated flight, lying on his bed, and the original print has written on it, 'Wickam has a wee drappie!' Hopefully the photo was not taken on the day in question.

Incidents involving the DH.9 began to happen on regular basis, and on 12 August, D2924 overshot the runway, side-slipped, then crashed into a field. Although the aeroplane caught fire, the two crew – Lieutenant Ratcliffe and Sergeant Mechanic Alderton – suffered only minor injuries. One modification made to the DH.9 was to extend the exhaust pipe down beneath the cockpit above the lower wing. That was done to carry the fumes further away from the cockpit and improve visibility, and it also reduced the amount of fumes from the castor oil used to lubricate the engines that the crew breathed in.

On 15 August, another aircraft was lost when Camel F1518 of the newly formed No. 219 Squadron at Manston crashed into the sea. However, that incident had a happy ending because its pilot survived and was picked up out of the water by Short seaplane N2635. That was one advantage of having a seaplane station close to a land-based unit, and a number of pilots were saved by the seaplanes based at Westgate.

There was a similar incident to that involving Flight Cadet Wickam when, on 22 August, another DH.9 from No. 203 TDS also spun into the ground from approximately 500 feet The aeroplane, D2830, was a write-off, but fortunately the pilot, Flight Cadet Marshall, was only slightly injured.

September was a bad month when the Air Council decided to move both Nos 55 and 203 TDS out of Manston. The loss of its personnel and aeroplanes would have made a big difference at Manston, especially after the loss of the Handley Page Training Flight to Stonehenge. Number 55 TDC was moved to Marham, while No. 203 TDS went to Sedgeford. The whole structure of the RFC and the RNAS was going through a number of radical changes, and those taking place at Manston were just part of a much bigger picture.

CHAPTER 7

The Growth of Manston

Among the unique features of RAF Manston were the legendary underground hangars at two sites on the airfield, one at Alland Grange to the west, and the other beside the Margate road close to the airfield boundary. They are unique because there is no record of any other airfield, military or civil, ever having such buildings.

Over the years there has been a lot of debate about whether the hangars were actually built underground or just sunk beneath the ground, with ramps that allowed aircraft access to them. Some reports state that the hangars were built out of concrete and steel and were 105 feet long and 90 feet wide with a clearance of sixteen feet by the hangar doors, but the exact measurements are not known. The bulk of the work on the hangars was carried out by the Air Service Construction Corps under the command of Captain Fann of the Royal Navy. Major Lillicrap of the Royal Engineers was also involved in the excavation of the hangars, which were built to protect large aeroplanes such as the Handley Page machines.

Few photographs of the hangars exist, but those few that do, show the sides being built by bricks that were later covered and supported with a wooden structure. The roof of corrugated-iron sheet was shaped into a shallow arch held up by metal trestles running across the hangars and supported on each side by the brick walls. The photographs seem to prove that the hangars were 'sunken' and not genuinely underground, but it is possible that the roof was covered over with soil or other forms of camouflage material.

Apart from the limited photographic evidence, there are only a few documentary references to the underground hangars, one of them in the Manston Diary just dated 1918 but probably written in February that year. It notes a very large workshop that was built as a repair base for the Handley Page machines. There were also two 'V' type hangars described as being 200 feet by 1,008 feet, one four-bay hangar for Handley Page machines, fourteen Bessonneau hangars, and five underground hangars under construction.

A subsequent excavation of the Alland Grange site found a series of concrete pillars two feet square and three feet high, with metal bolts protruding from the top to suggest that they were used to support the structure of the building such as the roof. Whether the roof was a permanent feature or a canvas one, like those of the Bessonneau hangars, is also open to debate. Of the two sites it is thought that only the ones at Alland Grange were finished before the end of the war, and that the one on the Margate road was never finished.

There are a huge number of myths and tales about Manston's underground hangars, most of them totally unsubstantiated. They originate mainly from rumour-mongers who have posted them on the internet, but they themselves have little or no knowledge about the airfield and have never served there in the RAF. One of the most popular myths claims that there are a number of Burmese Air Force Spitfires buried in crates in one of the hangars. Strangely enough, as I wrote this account in April 2012, rumours had spread through the British media that a large number of Spitfires had been found in Burma. It was claimed that they had been put into crates at the end of the war and buried in the ground for fear that they could be used by other foreign powers. The person who began the rumours about them being buried at Manston seemingly not only got the wrong airfield but the wrong country!

There are also various stories and tales about secret underground passages and caves around the airfield. The claims that they exist in themselves cannot be dismissed, and when I was stationed at Manston I heard various rumours about such things, but never anything that could be substantiated or supported by fact. However, the area around the station at Manston is riddled with underground passages and caves, so there may be some truth in them. The question is whether they were used for military purposes or are just connected to Thanet's notorious past.

There is an old chalk quarry called Smugglers Leap just outside the airfield boundary opposite the former Prospect Inn (now the Holiday Express Inn) and which has long-standing connections with smuggling. There are also at least two caves with tunnels that lead to the beach in nearby Cliffsend, and there are many others along the Thanet coast that have further connections with the notorious smuggler Joss Snelling and his gang.

In Ramsgate there are tunnels left over from an electric railway that were used as air-raid shelters during the Second World War. The fact that such an official source as the *Royal Air Force Journal* mentions that a number of caves existed at Manston, and that some were enlarged and used as shelters, supports the claims that they existed. Most RAF stations have their secrets, but it seems that Manston just happens to have more than most.

There are several reasons for that, including the rich history of the local area with the Roman fort of Richborough just down the road, as well as the 'secret port' at Stonar (Richborough) that was established during the Great

War. Then there is St Augustine's Cross in Cliffsend, where the saint is said to have landed in AD 597, and nearby 'Bloody Point', the scene of a great battle on the River Stour between the Vikings and Saxons in AD 851. There is no doubt that the Isle of Thanet is a very special place, and the airfield at Manston is another part of its unique history.

By mid-1918, RAF Manston was developing into the form and shape it would retain for many years into the future, and its size had grown to cover 650 acres. On the main camp, row upon row of long, low-level, whitewashed buildings were built to accommodate the increasing number of personnel posted in, until at the peak of its strength, Manston had approximately 2,500 personnel. On the west site of the station there was an Anglican church and close to the church was a parade ground, under which shelters were built to provide protection for 4,000 men. The shelters were built quite close to the surface and, some years later, part of the parade ground collapsed into the ground. Fortunately there was nobody on it at the time.

Manston's role as a training station was strengthened in September 1918 with the arrival of No. 2 School of Observers, equipped with various different types of aircraft but utilising a number of DH.4s and Avro 504s. This was a large unit, effective from the 14th, with 125 aircraft divided up into five Flights, and 2,539 personnel including some members of the WRAF, under the overall command of Lieutenant-Colonel A. C. Bishop. The personnel were made up mainly from surplus from the disbandment of the two Training Depot Stations, and it was planned that at least 500 trained observers would be created every month.

In October 1918, Bishop was appointed as the Commanding Officer of Manston. Of all the COs of Manston up to this point, least is known about the man who also commanded No. 2 School of Observers. It is known that on 8 February 1917, he was listed as being at the School of Military Aeronautics, Reading, and then went on to command No. 7 Armament School at Uxbridge. He was mentioned in despatches in 1918, holding the rank of Captain but acting temporary Lieutenant-Colonel for having rendered valuable service to the war effort. At the end of 1918, he is mentioned in *Flight* magazine as having re-mustered from the Berkshire Yeomanry in the Territorial Force Reserve and holding the rank of 2nd Lieutenant in the RAF, acting as temporary Lieutenant and being an assistant instructor graded as an equipment officer. A year later, in November 1919, he was mentioned again in *The London Gazette* as Captain A. C. Bishop, Lieutenant-Colonel in the RAF, promoted to the rank of Captain. How he could be a Lieutenant-Colonel (RAF rank of Wing Commander from 1919) and also a Captain who was promoted to Captain is very confusing, to say the least!

By September, operations at both Manston and Westgate had begun to wind down, and the number of sorties flown in that month by the seaplanes from Westgate amounted to just nine patrols. Lieutenant Frederick Calhoun Vincent, who had been one of the two Camel pilots from Manston who had escorted the ill-fated seaplanes on 18 July, attempted to make amends for the losses that day. On 29 September, he observed a couple of enemy seaplanes loitering in the Thames Estuary and gave chase as far as the Kentish Knock before losing them in the gloom and returning to Manston without getting his revenge.

Just a few months later, Vincent was posted to Russia as part of the RAF contingent to support the Russian White Army. In January 1919, he was mentioned in despatches for his work with the British Military Mission and the Latvian Army, and in January 1920, he was awarded the DFC.

Another unique feature of RAF Manston was that it had its railway own line, with trains running on a spur from the main line connecting London and Dover. The idea of a railway link had first been mooted on 11 December 1917, but had then been abandoned primarily because of the cost. It was common practice for the service to name air stations after the nearest railway station, and if that had been the case, RNAS Manston would probably have been called RNAS Birchington. That was because Birchington was where the line to Manston began, at a spur approximately 35 chains to the west of the railway station. Constructed by the Royal Engineers, the railway was used to transport both materials and supplies to Manston during what was probably its biggest period of growth. Even today, many of the roads around Manston, with the exception of the A2, are narrow and unsuitable for the continuous use of large vehicles with loads of aggregate and cement. One can only imagine what the roads were like in 1918.

The line into Manston was called a light railway, but the engines that ran along it were anything but light and were the usual ones that serviced the South Eastern & Chatham Railway. One of the regular engines used on the line was the 'E' class tank engine No. 1431, weighing 5 tons 16 cwt empty and 6 tons 17½ cwt fully loaded. It was one of six such types built by Andrew Barclay of Kilmarnock on instructions from the Admiralty for engines that were to be used by the Air Service Construction Corps and was delivered on 19 February 1918. The railway line was just three-and-a-quarter miles long, and a station was built at Manston along with the usual support facilities such as a water tower, sidings and a signalbox.

The Manston link joined the North Kent line on the 'up' side to the west of Birchington, close to the site of the Birchington 'A' signalbox that was later demolished in 1929. The line went across the fields towards the Canterbury road which it crossed some 80 yards west of King Edward Road, before carrying on across the fields to the Acol road which it crossed just below a short firtree-lined road that led to the Cotton Powell estate. It actually skirted around the estate (now Quex Park), running close to the Sparrow Castle water pumping station and then ran parallel to the Manston road, crossing the road that led to Cheeseman's Farm before going on to the airfield. The terminus at Manston was close to Pouce's farmhouse where there was a long platform and sidings.

At the Minnis Bay (Birchington) end of the line was another long siding in which the carriages were shunted from the main line in preparation for being taken to Manston. It has been said that a small steam engine was used for that purpose, but occasionally mainline engines were deployed for that job. It is interesting to note that the line had been built on a bed of cinders and used a new American style of construction known as 'flat-bottom'. This meant that instead of the line being bolted to the sleepers, it was 'dogged' or clipped. There were no signals at all on the line, and all the points were hand worked.

It must be emphasised that the primary use of the line was to carry supplies, such as petrol, aeroplanes and other goods to Manston, and that was done normally in wagons especially adapted for freight. Although service personnel could be issued with tickets, they could travel on the line only when coaches were available. Most of the coaches that were connected were linked up at Birchington, but occasionally passenger coaches were connected at the Manston end, although it is claimed that most passengers were carried in the guard's van.

One of the regular drivers was Leonard Hosken, who had been involved with steam of one form or another for most of his life and had previously driven steam lorries. He was the regular driver of engine No. 1431 that routinely worked the line, although he may have driven another engine, No. 422, an 'o' type engine that was used by the Air Service Construction Corps.

Built onto the side of the station at Manston was another large building – the power station, which used huge amounts of coal. The coal was also carried into Manston by the railway, so avoiding the logistical problem of large lorries driving along the narrow local lanes. The power station generated electricity for the whole airfield, and for a military unit such as Manston to produce its own electricity was a very forward-thinking and innovative idea in 1918.

Manston had not only a Pilots' Pool but also a heated indoor swimming pool for the use of officers and those from the ranks. The Pilots' Pool at Manston was turned into a Demobilisation Centre during October in anticipation of the end of the war. Patrols continued to be flown from both Manston and Westgate, but there was considerably less enemy activity. In October, the German seaplane base at Zeebrugge was evacuated, much to the relief of all those who had seen the seaplanes in action. The main units at Zeebrugge, 'See 1', had caused a lot of problems for the RNAS and the RAF, and were credited with destroying twenty-six Allied aeroplanes and two airships.

As the date of the Armistice approached, patrols continued to be flown from Westgate and aircraft were mainly sent out on mine-searching patrols to locate those that had been laid by both the Allies and the Germans. In late October, a number of mines were spotted drifting close to the South Knock, and sometimes they were used for target practice by surface craft as it was too dangerous for an aeroplane to try and blow them up. They were left mainly to the experienced crews of drifters and minelayers to deal with.

When the Armistice was signed on 11 November, and after four years of war, the Manston Diarist was quite conservative with his comments, the most significant of which being, 'The War Flight ceased in November 1918 and the Pilots' Pool was in 1919 turned into a Demobilisation Centre and gradually closed down.' The RAF began to reduce its strength almost immediately, but there was a note of caution because this was not the end of the war. That was not to happen for another six months, but the number of units at Manston was the lowest since 1916, and No. 219 Squadron was the only one left.

On 9 November, the *Thanet Advertiser and Echo* ran with the headline, 'The Epidemic. Influenza Comes To Thanet'. The story stated that although Thanet had not suffered so violently as other areas of the country, there were many local cases and doctors were experiencing a busy and anxious time. On the same day that the newspaper was published, nine members of the RAF died of influenza or one of its related conditions such as pneumonia.

CHAPTER 8

The Lean Years

On 17 February 1919, the Air Navigation Bill was receiving its second reading in Parliament. This was a vital piece of legislation upon which the future of British civil aviation depended. General Seely, the Under-Secretary of State for Air, was the Minister with the responsibility of guiding the Bill through Parliament.

There were a number of concerns and questions asked about whether individuals should be allowed to build their own aeroplanes, and controls on aeroplanes flying over private property. The question was also raised as to who was responsible if an aeroplane crashed and killed someone on the ground, and would one have to prove negligence? The purpose of the Bill that was passed into law was to sanction the use of civil aviation and regulate the use of aeroplanes, the responsibility for which fell to the Board of Trade.

From 20 April 1919, it was a requirement that all civil aeroplanes must carry a registration serial on them so that they could be easily identified. Civil flying was authorised to begin from 1 May. Aeroplanes that carried passengers were obliged to provide a Certificate of Airworthiness. The Civil Register that was adopted was based on radio call signs that had been agreed at the Radio Telegraphic Conference in 1913. The only problem was that the register and call signs were not just for the use of aeroplanes but were for anyone who had a radio.

To begin with, aeroplanes from the UK used a temporary register with the letter 'K' followed by a number. It could be claimed that the first civil flight in England was made by a former RAF DH.9, serial number C6054, when it flew from Hounslow to Bournemouth on 1 May. It was later allocated the serial, G-EAAA but it crashed before it could ever display that registration. The United Kingdom had been allocated the identification letter 'K' followed by a number and C6054 was given the registration 'K-100', but within a few months that would change.

Despite the introduction into law of civil aviation, when the Air Ministry was approached by the Avro Aviation Company in June to establish a local flying centre at Manston, it was refused. That was despite the intervention of General

Seely, who had recommended that the flying centre should be allowed. There were still two RAF units at Manston in the form of No. 219 Squadron and No. 2 School of Observers, so permission may have been refused because of a conflict between military and civil interests. As a result of that decision, a piece of ground outside the station near Cheeseman's Farm had to be used, and many of the local residents who could afford it got their first experience of flying. The company was operated by Captain Duncan Davies, who was the Head of Flying at Brooklands and Lympne, and Captain Phillips of Cornwall Aviation, who also promoted Avro aeroplanes. The head reporter for the *Isle of Thanet Gazette* wrote that he had 'never enjoyed anything so much in all my life'. He and the editor went up for 20 minutes and during that time they not only experienced the sensation of straight and level flight but had also looped the loop no fewer that four times.

Not only was there competition between civil and military aviation but also between the RAF and the Royal Navy. William Joynson-Hicks MP, who had taken part in the debate on the Air Navigation Bill, posed a question to the First Lord of the Admiralty, wanting to know if an Air Department existed in the Admiralty and, if so, why? The First Lord replied that there was an Air Division that co-operated with the RAF on air operations with the Fleet, but it was manned by RAF officers. Over a year after the amalgamation of the RFC and the RNAS, some aspects of the merger still seemed to be causing frustration and some parties were obviously not happy with the fact that the Navy was still involved with aerial warfare.

With the end of the war, there were demands from the civilian population to get back to normal. It was not only those who had had their land requisitioned who complained, but the general public who were unhappy about restrictions enforced by the military that affected their everyday lives. One such complaint that affected those living in the area around Manston was that the Sandwich to Margate road was still closed at Stonar, and questions were asked in the House of Commons on three occasions (5 March, 15 April, 16 April) as to when it would be open again to the public. The Government claimed that because valuable stores were being returned from France and were being stored at the Stonar camp, there was a need for it to remain closed for security reasons. Although local people were issued with passes as a concession, it still left many very unhappy.

There was a fatal accident in mid-Channel on 9 May, when a Bristol F.2B Fighter crashed into the sea with the loss of three lives. One of the three airmen, Lieutenant Henry John Edgar Stokes, came from Margate and his family lived at The Lodge in Princess Gardens, Cliftonville. The aeroplane had departed from Ostend at 3 p.m. on a flight to No. 8 Air Acceptance Park at Lympne, but approximately 40 minutes later it developed engine trouble and the pilot, Sergeant Reginald Frank Fillmore, was unable to maintain control and prevent it from crashing into the sea. Lieutenant Llewellyn Lewis Meredith

Evans AFC made up the crew, all of whom were drowned, their bodies being recovered some time later, two miles north-east of Dungeness by the destroyer HMS *Teazer*. Twenty-four-year-old Stokes, the son of Mr and Mrs Edgar Stokes, was buried in Minster Cemetery. Evans was buried in Springfield Holy Trinity Cemetery, Essex, and twenty-three-year-old Fillmore (1479, awarded Gold Medal Serbia) was buried in St Mary's Cemetery at Osney, Oxford.

Although the failure to get permission to open a civilian flying centre at Manston was something of a setback, it did not prevent the development of civil aviation in Thanet and the setting up of an Aerial Post Service. The business was established by a renowned Australian pilot, the former Flight Lieutenant Sydney Pickles, who had been awarded Royal Aero Club Certificate No. 263 on 30 July 1912. Prior to joining the RNAS and becoming the leading instructor with the Admiralty, Pickles had been the Chief Test Pilot for Short Brothers, Blackburn Aviation, and Fairey Aviation.

On the same day that the Bristol Fighter crashed it was reported in the *Thanet Times* that on Saturday 3 May, Mr Pickles had delivered a letter by air that had been sent by the Australian High Commissioner in London to the Mayor of Margate, Alderman W. B. Reeve. The letter had been flown in a Fairey seaplane, G-EAAJ, a former Norwegian Air Force machine powered by a Rolls-Royce engine. After the seaplane had landed safely on the water at Margate, the letter was delivered to the Mayor at his residence on Canterbury Road at precisely 6 p.m. It was short and very polite:

Dear Mr Mayor,

I am sending this note to you by the hand of Flight Lieutenant Pickles, the young Australian, who has made his name by interesting and dangerous flying feat. He starts from London to-day to visit your celebrated city. I take the liberty of giving him this letter to deliver to you as a memento. I hope you will be good enough to accept it.

Yours faithfully,
Andrew Fisher.

The letter was the subject of much interest in the media and, as might be expected, the Mayor and Sydney Pickles had posed for a number of photos before the letter was actually handed over. The Mayor then handed Pickles a letter in reply to the High Commissioner, thanking him for his communication and saying that he felt most honoured to be chosen as the recipient of the first letter delivered by air in Margate. Pickles' activities no doubt promoted aviation in the eyes of the local people, but it was a business venture and the delivery of newspapers and letters by air was a very innovative enterprise.

Pickles was back in the news the following week after he had begun delivering the *Evening News* by air to the local area. With a wife and family to support, he was obviously trying hard to make a living. His wife, whom he had married in November 1916, was the former Miss Marks of Hampstead. The publicity was good for business, and it was reported that on Saturday the 10th there were novel scenes at Broadstairs when large crowds appeared to watch the arrival of Pickles' seaplane at 5.30 p.m. With the newspapers having been sealed in watertight covers, the intention was to drop them in the water, three local boatmen having been hired to recover them. However, Pickles' aim was good and the newspapers were parachuted onto dry land where the crowd got to them before the boatmen. The 2,000 copies were handed over to the distributing agent, but the cries of the news boys 'News by air' were not necessary as very soon all of them were sold.

On 24 May, there was another fatality at Manston when Air Mechanic 1st Class Walter Brisley died, although the circumstances of his death are not known. Brisley, who was a former member of the East Kent Regiment (2nd Battalion 'The Buffs') and the son of the late Daniel Brisley, was forty years old and came from Dover. He was buried in Margate Cemetery.

Possibly as a result of the intervention of General Seely earlier in the year, in June 1919, Manston was placed on the list of airfields open to both military and civilian aircraft and, as we have already noted, there was a demand at Manston. In July, there were further changes regarding civil aviation, with the UK adopting the prefix letter 'G', so the DH.9 K-100 became G-EAAB.

Despite the setbacks, it is interesting to note that, many years later, Manston did develop very strong connections with civil aviation and was the only RAF station to have civil airlines based within its boundaries (Air Ferry and Invicta Airways). How much that had to do with the declaration made in 1919 is anyone's guess, but it formed the basis of a strong bond between civil and military aviation.

The former RNAS station at Westgate was still operational, but by July 1919 it was the only one still carrying out mine-searching patrols and by then its days were numbered. The same month, the Commanding Officer, Major Livock, was among a number of officers from Manston and Westgate posted to Russia, so he did not oversee the running down and closure of the base. After being transferred to the RAF, he would, however, eventually reach the giddy heights of Group Captain and also make his name at a cricketer, playing both for the RAF and first class cricket for Middlesex, for whom he was both a batsman and wicket keeper.

Livock was replaced at Westgate by Captain Ronald Sykes DFC, who had earned the honour while flying with No. 201 Squadron on the Western Front. It is possible that Sykes flew what turned out to be the very last patrol from Westgate, on 25 July. Accompanied by Lieutenant Liddy, he flew N9001 from

A Handley Page transport aircraft at Manston during August 1920. G-EAPG had first been named *Newcastle* but it was later renamed *Duchess of York*. The occasion is believed to have been a works outing. The aircraft was written off in an accident at Pouix in France during July 1923. (*John Williams*)

the Kentish Knock to South Falls, returning via Foulness on a minesweeping patrol. Within a short while, Sykes followed Livock and was posted to Russia, and over the next six months Westgate's aeroplanes were dispersed to stations such as Calshot or Felixstowe before the final official closure notice was issued.

The first mention of a civil aeroplane at Manston is on 30 August 1919, and it was an Avro 536, G-EACG, owned by the A. V. Roe Company. The 536 was a new type of aeroplane that had had its first flight only in May that year, and it is known that it was one of two that had previously been used to give pleasure flights to members of the public at Southsea, the other one being G-EADC. The aeroplane, built and designed for the civil market, was fitted with a powerful 150 hp Bentley rotary engine and was capable of carrying four people. There had been a number of other fatal accidents involving the Avro 536 and on some models the fin had been modified to offset the torque of the powerful Bentley engine. It is believed that G-EACG had been moved to Thanet and had been giving pleasure flights in Margate, but except for the fact that the aeroplane crashed at Manston there are no details of those who might have been killed or injured.

Handley Page O/400 G-EAPJ was a frequent visitor at Manston in 1920, and on one occasion a group photo was taken of twenty people, including five women, who were about take a flight in the aircraft. It is understood that the occasion was the first Handley Page works outing from the factory at Cricklewood. The HP O/400 had originally been named *Newcastle*, but that was later changed to *Duchess of York*. It had first flown on 2 December 1919, and was in regular civil service for four years before it crashed near Poix in France in July 1923.

No. 2 School of Observers was disbanded at Manston in September 1919, but it was almost immediately replaced by No. 1 Observers School of Aerial Gunnery, which moved in from New Romney. It had been founded from an amalgamation of No. 1 (Auxiliary) School of Gunnery and No. 2 School of Observers. The unit had previously operated out of a little-known airfield on the Romney Marshes called Jesson, also known later as Littlestone. Its establishment was made up of 1,000 airmen; 400 airwomen; 300 NCOs and 400 officers.

Despite its title, which suggests that it only trained observers, it also trained pilots, and it was estimated that 400 pilots from each intake would qualify for their wings. As might be expected at any training establishment, there were a number of serious accidents and a number of students were killed while learning to fly. However, not all of them happened in the air. One of the strangest incidents occurred on the beach at New Romney and involved 2nd Lieutenant William Francis John Prince on what should have been a leisurely day swimming in the sea. Although it has been recorded that Prince was in the service of the Army, the Commonwealth War Graves Commission states that he was a member of the RAF. It seems that he had previously served with the 9th Battalion of the London Regiment but later re-mustered to the RAF.

On Thursday 30 May 1918, he and a number of other personnel were swimming off the coast of New Romney. What happened next is best described by the local newspaper report: 'Whilst bathing off the south Kent coast a man belonging to the RAF got too near a sea target when firing practice was in progress and was killed.' The exact circumstances of the incident have never been released, but it culminated with Prince being shot in the head. Whether he was working with the targets in the water and was on duty or was just taking a leisurely swim and got too close to the target is not known, but it was a tragic accident.

According to the information held in the records of the Commonwealth War Graves Commission, Prince was serving with No. 1 Observer School of Aerial Gunnery and was based at Manston. The unit was based at New Romney at the time of the incident and did not move to Manston for another year or so, but it is possible that Prince was accommodated there and was transported to New Romney when necessary. The twenty year old was buried in Chingford Mount Cemetery.

CHAPTER 9

The School of Technical Training

No. 1 School of Aerial Gunnery closed down in December 1919, and during the latter end of the year considerable time and administration was being committed towards the formation of the School of Technical Training. Compared to the heady days of 1917, the establishment at Manston was reduced to just one unit consisting of the small number of Camels and DH.9s of No. 219 Squadron. Wing Commander William Harold Primrose was appointed as the first Commandant of the Technical Training School in November 1919, but it would be another six months or so before its first batch of trainee airmen arrived and it became fully functional.

The following month, Wing Commander Primrose also took over command of the station, working with the Adjutant, Pilot Officer C. Fenn. Thirty-five-year-old Primrose, who had been educated at Kelvinside Academy and Glasgow University, had first joined the colours on 31 October 1903. That was when he had volunteered for the 4th Battalion Stirlingshire Volunteer Regiment. He later transferred to Princess Louise's Argyll and Sutherland Highlanders before resigning his commission in November 1909.

Primrose had been awarded his Royal Aero Club Certificate, No. 1779, on 22 September 1915, before being commissioned into the RFC as a Flight Sub-Lieutenant on 18 October that year. By 1917, he was serving in Egypt with No. 32 Wing (Reserve) and after returning to the Home Establishment he was awarded a permanent commission as a Lieutenant-Colonel (Wing Commander) on 1 August 1919. As was the tradition at Manston, the Commanding Officer was also put in command of another resident unit, and in Primrose's case it was the newly established School of Technical Training.

As Manston was still operational and increasingly taking on a very important training role, the seaplane station at Westgate was in decline and in January 1920, it was transferred from an Air Ministry List 'C' Station to a List 'E'. That meant that it was no longer to be used by the RAF, and it was passed over to the Government Property Disposal Board for the land and property to be sold at auction. On 7 February 1920, the station was officially closed with little or no ceremony and no publicity in the local newspapers. With the closure of Westgate, RAF Manston became a truly independent unit for the first time.

It was not just Westgate that was being closed down, however. No. 219 Squadron at Manston was disbanded on the same day and its Camels and DH.9s were made redundant. During its short existence, the squadron had not lost a single member of its personnel in any incident.

It had never been intended for the School of Technical Training to be based at Manston. Eastchurch had been the first choice of the Air Ministry, but although an initial establishment was raised at Eastchurch, it never materialised as a working unit. There must have been various arguments put forward among the powers that be, and according to a letter from the Inland Area HQ (1A/2475/Area O, dated 12 April 1920) the decision was made that the 'unit' at Manston should be called the School of Technical Training (Men). In the same letter it was stated that the unit at Eastchurch was to be called the Armament and Gunnery School. Subsequently the School at RAF Manston came formally into being in May 1920.

The role of the School of Technical Training was to train airmen in every trade that was available to those who joined the RAF, and initially it was divided into two sections. Carpenters, riggers and fabric workers were in one section, with drivers, machinists, acetylene welders and fitters in the other. The School was the first of its kind and was to remain one of the most important training units that ever existed in the years before the Second World War. It was established because a decision had been made to train men and boys separately, and while the technical training for boy entrants was to continue at Halton (what became known as the 'Brat School'), the facilities to train those who were categorised as men was moved to Manston.

The site of the former RNAS station at Westgate remained abandoned for a number of months and, surrounded by barbed-wire fencing, was said to have attracted a lot of attention from holidaymakers. Eventually an inventory of the station was carried out, and such items as building, huts and machinery were auctioned off in a sale organised by W. R. Noble & Co. on 15 December 1920.

In December 1920, a reunion was held at the Holborn Restaurant in Kingsway for those officers who had served at RNAS Westgate and many well-known names were present. Among them were Lieutenant-Colonel Robert Peel Ross, Major Ingram, Captain Oakey and Major Samson. It was proposed that the meeting should become an annual event, but the majority decided against this, wanting to remember everyone as they were then. A final chorus of 'Auld Lang Syne' was sung and the final chapter in the history of Westgate and No. 219 Squadron came to an end.

In January 1921, the Treasury was in communication with the Air Ministry about the acquisition of the airfield and the acreage that might be let to raise revenue. The Air Ministry stated that the only available area for letting was 80 acres, and that the maximum amount of rent that could be raised for the grazing land was 10s an acre. It also pointed out that the greater part of the airfield was not fenced in and that to let an area for grazing, there would have to be a considerable outlay to allow cattle to graze safely.

The only alternative way to raise revenue according to the Air Ministry was to let an area for the cultivation of crops, but it pointed out that it would seriously limit the area available for aircraft to land in an emergency. It said that a Flying Training School was shortly to be based at Manston, and that ample landing facilities saved aircraft from crashing and consequently that saved money. It claimed that preventing a single crash would more than compensate for money raised by letting off parts of the aerodrome. Despite the reassurances given, in December 1917 the future of RAF Manston was anything but secure, and the arguments about its role were to rumble on for many more years.

The first few months of 1921 was a busy time at Manston. A number of alterations were made to the station's buildings in order to deal with its changing role as a permanent RAF base. Airmen's Married Quarters were built for the first time in early 1921 for Warrant Officers and NCOs, the Officers' Mess, Cadet quarters and Airmen's huts situated close to the former War Flight site being converted for that purpose. The work was carried out by carpenters, both instructors and pupils, from the School of Technical Training and the first occupants moved in during May.

Monday 21 February 1921 was a memorable day for RAF Manston, when it was visited and inspected by Air Marshal Sir Hugh Trenchard, the so-called 'Father of the Royal Air Force'. The Air Marshal was honoured by a march past of the Station Headquarters building, where he took the salute before inspecting airmen and senior NCOs from the various departments of the station. The main section he inspected was of those airmen, both trainees and instructors, belonging to the School of Technical Training. What Trenchard thought about Manston, and whether it reached the high standards of dress and discipline that he expected, would only have been for the ears of a number of senior officers.

It is understood that it was during his visit to Manston that he first mooted the idea of establishing the University Air Squadrons and that the airfield at Manston would be a good place for them to train and hold their summer camps. However, it would be another four years before Cambridge became the first such unit to be formed, with the Oxford Squadron forming a few days later. Through Trenchard's influence, the University Air Squadrons were later to form close ties with Manston and their summer camps became a regular event.

With the loss of No. 219 Squadron and the School of Aerial Gunnery, for the first time since the station had opened in 1916, there were no permanent flying units based at Manston. There would still have been a lot of activity from those officers and airmen from the School of Technical Training, but aerial activity would have been drastically reduced and it must have seemed a large and lonely place for some of those that remained.

In May 1921, because of what was described as a 'great influx' of recruits at the RAF Depot at Uxbridge, many of them were posted to the School of Technical Training at Manston for training in drill and discipline. As a result, the school was divided up into three sections, with No. 1 being made the Disciplinary Section and Nos 2 and 3 for those airmen receiving technical training. A number of short service commissioned officers were also posted to Manston for instruction in administration, drill, and discipline. Many of them were former RAF officers who had returned to the service on short-term contracts, or Army officers who had been seconded to the RAF for a period of four years. During that time they would undergo training as pilots and at the end of it be posted to Army Co-operation units.

On 24 May, Wing Commander Primrose performed his duty as Commanding Officer of the station and confirmed its close ties to the local population when he unveiled the war memorial in the village of Manston. The memorial had the names of fourteen local servicemen on it, including two brothers: twenty-five-year-old Lance Corporal William John Howland of the Royal Engineers, and twenty-one-year-old Private Herbert Howland of the 7th Battalion of the East Kent Regiment ('The Buffs'). No members of the RFC or RAF were mentioned on the war memorial, many of those named having served with the East Kent Regiment and all of them having served in the ranks.

Perhaps the most poignant name inscribed on the memorial was that of Private Ernest Joseph Lodge of the Machine Gun Corps (Heavy). He was the son of Thomas and Elizabeth Lodge who were the landlord and landlady of the Jolly Farmer public house that was, and still is, just across the road from the war memorial. Every time they stepped out of their door they were faced with the memorial and its reminder of their twenty-year-old son who had been killed on 20 April 1917 and buried near Arras.

During 1921, the expansion of the RAF and the other two services was seriously affected when Prime Minster Lloyd George appointed a committee to find ways of making savings. The Chairman was Sir Eric Geddes and his subsequent recommendations were that huge cuts should be made to the Defence Budget. Overall, it was cut by 42 per cent, but compared to the cuts made to the Army and Navy, the RAF got off lightly. However, both Manston and the RAF generally suffered as a result.

The first copy of RAF Manston's journal *The Airman* was published in June 1921, edited by Flight Lieutenant Saville. The journal was to prove very popular with its readers, but the publication relied heavily on a small number of personnel and that was to prove its undoing.

It was not until September 1921, after Manston had been bereft of regular aerial activity for the best part of a year and a half, that, as stated in its letter to the Treasury at the beginning of the year, No. 6 Flight Training School arrived at Manston. The unit had originally been formed in No. 3 Group on 26 April 1920, at Spittlegate in Lincolnshire, from No. 39 TDS.

At Manston, No. 6 FTS was based in the buildings on the Ramsgate side of the airfield, previously known as the War Flight side, because that is where that unit had been formed back in 1916. Wing Commander H. L. Reilly DSO is noted as being the original Commanding Officer of No. 6 FTS, and the future AOC of Fighter Command, Squadron Leader Sholto Douglas, was the Chief Flying Instructor. The unit operated a variety of aircraft, with the main types being the Avro 504, the Bristol Fighter and the Vickers Vimy bomber. Many of the pupils of No. 6 FTS were officers on short service commissions from all three services.

The Vickers Vimy, a twin-engine, long-range heavy bomber that had first flown in November 1917, was the successor to the Handley Page V/1500 heavy bomber. It was made most famous by the feat of Alcock and Brown when they flew across the Atlantic in the type in June 1919. The Vimy was in RAF service from 1919 until 1925, and to begin with it was fitted with a number of different types of engines. The type best known as fitted to the Vimy Mk IV was the Rolls-Royce Eagle engine which powered the aircraft to speeds of up to 98 mph.

One of the Squadron Commanders on No. 6 FTS was Squadron Leader John Tremayne Babington, who over the years had been posted in and out of both Westgate and Manston on a number of occasions. After moving from Manston with the Handley Page Flight to Stonehenge in 1917, Babington had carried out several different roles. After being graded as a Lieutenant-Colonel and awarded a permanent commission in August 1919, he had spent some time in Germany as a member of the Commission of Aeronautical Control. In 1920, Babington had been removed from the Navy List and awarded a commission in the RAF. Like a number of other senior officers, he had been classed as supernumerary and in August 1921, was posted to the Depot at Uxbridge. However, on 29 August, he was posted back to Manston as a Squadron Commander on No. 6 FTS.

Among the instructors at No. 6 FTS was Flight Lieutenant Arthur Stanley Gould Lee, who had originally been commissioned into the Sherwood Foresters Regiment and, over the years, would rise to the rank of Air Vice-Marshal. He had been turned down for flying training on a number of occasions, initially because he did not hold a Royal Aero Club Certificate, but later on for various other reasons. Lee later became a great advocate for the wearing of parachutes, disagreeing with those in authority who claimed that, if issued with them, pilots would use them rather than pressing home their attacks. His argument was that if they knew they had a chance of escaping death, they would be *more* likely to press home their attacks, a point later proved in the Second World War. Lee remained at Manston for a number of months before being transferred as an instructor to No. 2 FTS.

In September 1921, reserves of officers and airmen were mobilised at Manston when a railway and docks strike threatened to bring the South East to a halt. There was civil unrest in London, particularly in Poplar, where local councillors had refused to collect precepts on behalf of various cross-London authorities because of the high rates of poverty. A number of councillors were imprisoned, and at least five women were jailed in Holloway, while twenty-five men were sent to Brixton Prison. A total of 80 officers and 589 airmen were among those mobilised at Manston, but the situation began to calm down when those imprisoned were released, so they were not required.

There are various dates given for when the parade ground collapsed, but it is noted in the Operational Record Book that a new parade ground was constructed and a flagstaff erected in September 1921. Whether this was because of subsidence is not known, but it is also noted that three years later the parade ground collapsed and had to be rebuilt again!

As might be expected of a Flying Training Unit, there were a number of accidents involving aircraft from No. 6 FTS and the most serious occurred on 3 October 1921. A Vickers Vimy, F9157, was taking off when it spun around and crashed to the ground killing all five airmen on board. In terms of lives lost, it was the most serious incident that had ever happened at Manston. In the past, most accidents had involved a single aircraft and the loss of one or two lives, but it was to be expected that with the introduction into service of aeroplanes like the Handley Page and Vickers Vimy, a single incident would result in many more deaths. The most probable cause of the accident was later thought to be engine failure, causing the aircraft to swing on take-off.

The make-up of the crew of F9157 suggests that the ill-fated sortie was not a training flight but either a 'jolly' for the ground crew or a test flight on which those mechanics who had worked on the aeroplane had been invited to take part. There was a long-standing unofficial tradition in the Air Force that mechanics and riggers who had worked on an aeroplane should be taken on the test flight to prove their workmanship and faith in their abilities.

Twenty-two-year-old Flying Officer Leslie Wallis Beal from Frome was the pilot, but there were another four airmen on board. They were twenty-one-year-old Aircraftman 1st Class Terence Curteis, nineteen-year-old Aircraftman 2nd Class Albert Arthur Revell, twenty-one-year-old Aircraftman 2nd Class Robert John Reeves, and twenty-year-old Aircraftman 2nd Class William Edward Thrupp. All five airmen were buried together in St John's Cemetery, Margate.

In November 1921, Wing Commander Primrose was relieved of the role

The burning wreckage of Vickers Vimy F9157 from Number 6 Flying Training School that crashed on 3 October 1921 after going into a spin during take-off. Its crew were killed and buried in Margate's St John Cemetery. (*John Williams & Peter Laudi*)

of Commanding Officer of Manston by Wing Commander Joseph Herbert Arthur Landon OBE, DSO. Landon came from Shenfield in Essex and was the son of a retired Colonel who had joined the Army in 1905 and served as a 2nd Lieutenant in the 4th battalion of the Essex Regiment. By 1908, he had risen to the rank of Captain and, having always taken a keen interest in aviation, learned to fly at Brooklands in April 1913, being awarded Royal Aero Club Certificate No. 458.

Landon had flown operationally for the first time with No. 5 Squadron which was then equipped with the Vickers Gunbus, but after returning to the Home Establishment, in October 1915, he suffered serious injuries when his aeroplane suffered an engine failure and dived straight into the ground from 50 feet. His injuries included severe bruising and a deep puncture of his left tibia, but by early 1916 he had returned to flying and was posted as an instructor at the Central Flying School.

After being promoted to Squadron Commander in October 1916, Landon was appointed as the Commanding Officer of No. 41 Squadron and took the unit to France where it suffered heavy losses. In June 1917, it lost four pilots who were killed in enemy action, another two were wounded, and two more were taken as prisoners of war. Landon was awarded the DSO, and in August he relinquished his command and returned to the Home Establishment.

In June 1918, Landon returned to France with the rank of Wing Commander and became a Brigade Commander, but was later seriously injured when his staff car was bombed by an enemy aircraft. The driver was killed but Landon survived, although he was seriously injured and spent some time recovering in No. 14 General Hospital. From 1921 until 1923, and during his time at Manston, Landon was involved with the Air Ministry's Design Department, but his exact role is not known.

Four years earlier, a local newspaper had claimed that Thanet had escaped the influenza epidemic, but early in 1922 there was a serious outbreak at RAF Manston. It was blamed on the fact that for some reason, probably financial, inoculations had not been carried out as planned. Airmen were consequently confined to the camp, and the Medical Officer, Flight Lieutenant Barr-Simm, was personally affected, as he lost his wife who died of the virus. It was not on the same scale as a few years earlier at the end of the First World War, but it was serious enough to cause a number of fatalities.

During 1922, Wing Commander Primrose remained at Manston in the role of a supernumerary officer working with the Armoured Car Detail, which was under the overall control of the School of Technical Training. It is claimed that the members of his Armoured Car Unit were a tough bunch of men, with some of them having served in Ireland as what were known as 'Black and Tans'. A paramilitary unit employed by the Royal Irish Constabulary, it was made up mainly of veterans of the Great War. Shortly after they had received their brand new Lancia armoured cars, some members of the unit apparently decided to drive up to London to have a night out on the town. Eventually they were all rounded up and returned to Manston to face disciplinary charges, but they were probably treated lightly because very soon they would going overseas to a hot, distant and dangerous part of the world.

The School of Technical Training was in No. 1 Group but under the overall control of HQ Inland Area based at Uxbridge. Units at Hawkinge and Kenley, and the Gunnery School at Eastchurch, were also part of No. 1 Group and controlled by Uxbridge.

At the beginning of April 1922, No. 6 FTS, which had latterly been under the control of the School of Technical Training, was disbanded. For the second time in four years this left Manston without a permanently based flying unit, and the decision was almost certainly made as a result of what was known as the Geddes axe, a policy for the reduction of public expenditure. Although there was considerable activity from the section of the School of Technical Training and the occasional visiting aircraft, the airfield as such had very few movements.

Most of the personnel from No. 6 FTS remained at Manston and were posted to the School of Technical Training, at least until they received postings to other units. The School was the saviour of RAF Manston, and by early 1922 there were over 1,000 trainees under instruction. As a result of such a dramatic increase in its establishment, an additional fourth section was formed for pupils under technical instruction.

Early in 1922, *The Times* newspaper had published a report claiming that the French Air Force possessed a fleet of aircraft 600-strong, whereas the RAF had barely a quarter of that number. The French were still considered to be a potential enemy, and the report led to the setting up of the Air Defence of Great Britain in June. The organisation was to consist of no fewer than fifty-two squadrons to be divided into 'Fighter' and 'Bomber' sections. It was a huge project that would take several years to complete and 'kick start' the expansion of the RAF,

Wing Commander Primrose, along with twenty officers and a hundred airmen of the Armoured Car Unit, was posted from Manston to the former Turkish territory of Iraq in September 1922. To begin with, Primrose was posted to HQ Iraq, but in November he took over command of the Armoured Car Unit and was not destined to return to Britain until 1925.

In April 1923, Manston was inspected by the Secretary of State for Air, Sir Samuel Hoare, the Conservative MP for Chelsea, who had taken over the position from Frederick Guest in 1922. Hoare held the position of Secretary of State for Air on two occasions: from October 1922 to January 1924, and from November 1924 to June 1929. In 1924, he had handed over to Lord Thomson, as he did in 1929 when Hoare became the Secretary of State for India.

Such is the power of music, particularly bagpipes, that a pipe and drums band was formed at Manston in April 1923. The origins of the band are not known, but it may well have been organised and influenced by a number of homesick Scottish airmen. It was, however, noted in the records that the band was a great asset in marching airmen to and from their duties in the workshops.

One distinguished officer who was posted to the School of Technical Training at Manston in August 1923 was an ace pilot from the Great War, Flight Lieutenant John Oliver Andrews, who had been credited with twelve victories. Andrews, who came from Manchester, had been commissioned into the Royal Scots Guards in October 1914, but re-mustered to the RFC in 1915 and was awarded Royal Aero Club Certificate No. 1924 at Le Crotoy in France. He had been involved in many distinguished actions, including one on 27 April 1916, when he got the better of German ace Max Immelmann and damaged his aeroplane, filling it full of bullet holes.

Andrews was probably best associated with No. 24 Squadron, although he also served on No. 66, No. 70 (on which he was a Flight Commander) and No. 209 Squadron, which was his first command. He also served on Nos 220 and 221 Squadrons, commanding the latter in Russia in support of the White Army. In 1920, he attended Cambridge University, and immediately before being posted to Manston he had been studying at London University. There was no doubt that his experience and knowledge were valuable assets to the School of Technical Training.

By 1923, RAF Manston was a thriving part of a community that was not just confined to the airfield site but had spread to various parts of the local area in the parish of St Lawrence. Local records show that families of both airmen from the ranks and senior NCOs were living in places such as Clifton Road and the High Street in St Lawrence. Leading Aircraftman John Galloway lived at 2 Clifton Road with his wife Ethel Rosa Ann and their young son John, who had been born on 8 April 1923. Corporal Alfred Doyle lived at 4 High Street, St Lawrence, with his wife Margaret Mary Helen. William Thomas and his wife lived at 52 High Street, and the point that St Lawrence was a very mixed and military-minded community was proven by the fact that he was a former Army officer. On the station itself such a mixture of ranks was not allowed, and both Officers and Warrant Officers had their own separate quarters.

By 1924, former Lieutenant Spenser Grey, who twelve years earlier had claimed the distinction of being the first airman to land in Thanet, was no longer actively involved with flying. He had been injured in a number of aviation-related accidents and, after the Armistice, declared that he was giving up flying and took on a role on the Air Staff that involved liaising with the United States. The only exception to him having giving up flying occurred in September 1922, when he was sponsored by Winston Churchill to fly a Blackburn Kangaroo (G-EAMJ) in the King's Cup Air Race. However, when Grey realised that he would not make Glasgow in daylight, he was forced to withdraw from the race and retired at Newcastle.

It was announced in *Flight* magazine in February 1924 that Charles Rumney Samson, who had also been among the first airmen to land in Thanet in April 1912, was to take command of No. 1 Group at Kenley. Samson, like a number of other officers, had risen through the ranks in the twelve-year period since the event that had made news and gone down in aviation history, and was now an Air Commodore. The other officer from the RNAS who had also been among the first to land in Thanet, Lieutenant Arthur Longmore, had been promoted to Group Captain. At that point, he was on the Air Staff in Iraq, but he was about to return to the UK where he would be promoted to Air Commodore.

The Royal Navy was now about to get some of its control and authority back. After the Great War a number of squadrons had been allocated to both the Army and Navy to work in the role of co-operation with the RAF. This created a situation where often many of the pilots were from the RAF but the observers were from the Navy or Army. This came to a head on 1 April 1924 (the sixth anniversary of the founding of the RAF) when the Fleet Air Arm of the RAF was formed and the Royal Navy effectively got its own air force again that was more or less controlled by the Admiralty.

CHAPTER 10

The Birchington Incident

It was not until March 1924 that another permanent residential flying unit arrived at Manston, when No. 2 Squadron, equipped with the Bristol F.2B, was posted in from Andover in Hampshire. Since it had been equipped with what was commonly known as the Bristol Fighter, the squadron had been based at a number of different airfields, but after moving to Manston the unit was to have a long-term association with the station.

Number 2 Squadron (II Squadron) was the second oldest flying unit in the RFC, having been formed at Farnborough on 13 May 1912 with a mixture of types, including the B.E.1, Breguet 211, Blériot XI, Maurice Farman S.7, B.E.2, B.E.2b, and B.E.8. As it was the first squadron to cross the English Channel in August 1914, its personnel sometimes laid claim to it being the oldest unit, thus usurping No. 1 Squadron. During the First World War the squadron had been based at numerous airfields in France but had returned to the Home Establishment in February 1919, to be based at Bicester, by which time it was equipped with the FK.8. It had been re-equipped with the FE.2b while at Oranmore in Ireland, where it had been actively involved during the partition.

The role of No. 2 Squadron was Army Co-operation. Known in the RAF as 'Shiny Two', it was commanded by Squadron Leader Leslie Frederick Forbes MC, who had taken over the unit on 15 May 1922 from Squadron Leader A. J. Butler. It had been intended that Butler's successor should have been Squadron Leader Smythies, but he died just before he was due to take over command, although the cause of his death is not known. Commanding officers of No. 2 Squadron were typically known as 'Boss', and 'Boss' Forbes was a popular officer who had commanded the unit through difficult times in Ireland and also when its aircraft were dispersed over numerous airstrips and airfields. After leaving Ireland, No. 2 Squadron moved to Digby in Lincolnshire, then back to Aldergrove in Ireland, before returning to the mainland at Farnborough and Andover before being posted to Manston.

Soon after arriving at Manston, the unit proved the sporting abilities of its personnel by winning a number of football tournaments. These included the RAF Junior Soccer Cup and the 22 Group for RAF Manston. During the 1924–25 season RAF Manston competed in the Folkestone and District Senior League along with teams from Dover, the King's Own Regiment, Dover Marine Sports Club, Deal Town and the 3rd Battalion of the Royal Tanks Corps based at Lydd.

On 1 April 1924, the strength of its operational flying establishments at Manston was doubled when No. 3 Squadron was posted in from Gosport, equipped with the Sopwith Snipe fighter. The Snipe was meant to have been a replacement for the Camel. Powered by a 230 hp Bentley engine, it was the last RAF aircraft ever to be fitted with a rotary engine. Five of No. 3 Squadron's Snipes arrived at Manston in crates by rail and were duly assembled by a team of riggers in readiness for flight testing. Squadron Leader John C. Russell was the Commanding Officer of No. 3 Squadron, with Flight Lieutenant Claude Ridley as Flight Commander, and Flight Lieutenant Leonard H. Cocksey as Adjutant. Its establishment consisted of seven officers and fifty-three airmen. It was formed with a Headquarters Flight and one other called 'C' Flight.

However, even before the first Snipe got off the ground at Manston, an order arrived stating that the Snipes should be put back in their crates immediately and sent to Upavon in Wiltshire. It must have been quite confusing for both the officers and airmen to understand why the squadron should have to move out of Manston so quickly, but news quickly got out around the station as to what had happened.

The reason was a bureaucratic blunder in the Air Ministry. It had failed to realise that while the Snipes of No. 3 Squadron easily fitted into the huge war hangar at Manston with plenty of room to spare, the hangars available on another airfield were not big enough to accommodate the aircraft based there. The unit in question was No. 9 Squadron, which had recently been equipped with the Vickers Vimy and had just been posted to Upavon. It was very soon discovered that it was impossible to fit the large Vickers bombers into the small hangars at Upavon. Someone in the Air Ministry quickly made a decision to swap the two squadrons around and on 30 April, No. 9 Squadron moved to Manston, while No. 3 Squadron was posted to Upavon.

Of the seven officers of No. 3 Squadron that had been posted to Manston, one of them never arrived anyway: Flying Officer William E. Frederick, the Stores Officer, did not turn up at Upavon until June. He had only recently returned from Egypt and was on extended leave. Another officer, Flying Officer M. V. Nolan, got as far as Manston but he became seriously ill on 29 April and was admitted to the RAF Hospital at Finchley. He was not discharged until June, but he never got as far as Upavon because he was taken off flying duties and posted to the Depot at Uxbridge.

Number 9 Squadron had been disbanded after the First World War on 31 December 1919, but had re-formed at Upavon on 1 April, with a Headquarters Flight and one operational flight. At Manston the unit's role was to carry out night bomber duties associated with Home Defence, and it was under the control of No. 1 Group with its Headquarters at Kidbrooke.

There is an interesting story about an officer called Pilot Officer Grace who had flown the Snipe with No. 3 Squadron at Gosport and was not too keen on the aircraft because the rotary engine discharged a lot of lubrication in the form of castor oil. He claimed that even when he was sitting right down in his seat his neck and shoulders were covered in the stuff, and he was fed up with it. Although he hated the Snipe, he liked being at Manston and as soon as he heard that his squadron was about to move to Upavon he applied for a transfer to No. 9 Squadron. His move was authorised over the telephone by the Wessex Bombing Area, but when the signal arrived at Manston someone had put an extra '9' on it. As a result, he was posted to No. 99 Squadron at Bircham Newton in Norfolk, but although it was a long from where he wanted to be, at least it was equipped with the Vickers Vimy and he got away from the Snipe!

When No. 9 Squadron had re-formed on 1 April 1924, it had been under the command of Flight Lieutenant Victor Richard Gibbs DSC, who had learned to fly in March 1915 and was awarded Royal Aero Club Certificate No. 2565. He later handed over to Squadron Leader John Charles Quinnell DFC just before the move to Manston. The son of an Irish newspaper owner from Tralee, Quinnell had been commissioned into the Army as a Lieutenant in 1915, and in March that year had gained his Royal Aero Club Certificate, No. 1175.

Quinnell had re-mustered to the RFC in 1915, and had served as a pilot with No. 10 Squadron, and by 1916 he had been made a Flight Commander on No. 7 Squadron. He went on to gain a huge amount of experience and to command eight different squadrons, including Nos 27, 60, 83 and 97, as well as No. 3 Flight Training School at Scopwick. He had qualified as an Air Navigation Officer and immediately before being posted to No. 9 Squadron at Manston had spent nearly a year at the Staff College in Andover. It was hardly surprising that with all his experience, he was promoted to the rank of Wing Commander in August.

In July 1924, Group Captain Arthur Lowthian Godman CMG, DSO took over command of Manston and the role as Commandant of the School of Technical Training from Wing Commander Landon. The wing commander was posted to the Air Ministry in London.

Typical of those officers who were appointed to command RAF Manston, Godman had served in the military since before the Great War. Having joined the Militia of the Princess of Wales in 1895, he had over thirty years' experience to draw on. In 1898, he had been commissioned as a 2nd Lieutenant into the same regiment, and had served in Somaliland in military intelligence between 1904 and 1905. Having been seriously wounded in October 1914, he had been seconded to the RFC in November 1915, and by 1916 he had been appointed as a Brigade Major. After having been appointed to various other administrative positions he was awarded a permanent commission in August 1919 and promoted to the rank of Lieutenant-Colonel (Wing Commander).

In August 1919, Godman had become the Wing Commander at Headquarters South West Area, and in September that year he attended a staff course at the RAF College, Cranwell. In November, he passed out as a Staff Officer 1st Class and became the Assistant Commandant at the RAF College, before being posted to the Headquarters of the Air Staff in India in June 1920, arriving at Manston in July1924.

Shortly after Godman took over, Manston had a couple of high-profile visitors, the first of whom was the Crown Prince of Rumania, who inspected the workshop training area and was given a guard of honour. That was followed soon afterwards by a visit from the Chief of the Air Staff, Air Marshal Sir Hugh Trenchard, who carried out another inspection of the unit.

Squadron Leader Albert Peter Vincent Daly took over command of No. 9 Squadron in August 1924 after its establishment had been revised to include a Wing Commander and a Squadron Leader as a Flight Commander. The squadron's establishment was also raised to include two Flight Lieutenants and eight Flying Officers. Daly, originally from Ireland but brought up in Warwickshire, had learned to fly in March 1915 and began his flying career with No. 5 Reserve Aeroplane Squadron. He later served with No. 10 Squadron (RNAS) and during 1917 had been mentioned several times in RAF communiqués (No. 107).

One of the first accidents involving aircraft of No. 9 Squadron happened on 24 August, when Vickers Vimy F9182 crashed in a cornfield while taking off from Manston. It is claimed that the aircraft had suffered some damage to its starboard ailerons and its pilot was trying to go around again in order to make another landing. The Vimy had been delivered to the RAF on 27 August 1923, and taken on charge by No. 9 Squadron on 24 May 1924. It was one of those delivered as part of Contract No. 41752/23 and although nobody was badly injured, the aircraft was a write-off. The Vimy was being flown by Flight Lieutenant Martin and Pilot Officer Gary, with three other airmen from the ranks on board.

September 1924 was not a very good time for several reasons and this the time when the parade ground collapsed again. It was noted that had it done so during morning parade, there would have been considerable casualties. As noted earlier, the collapse was blamed on underground tunnels and shelters that had been built during the First World War and

Close-up view of the wreckage of 9 Squadron Vimy F9182, which sideslipped to the ground during take-off and crashed on 7 July 1924. (*John Williams & Peter Laudi*)

Another photo showing the wreckage of the 9 Squadron Vimy giving a more complete picture. Fortunately no one was seriously injured. (*John Williams & Peter Laudi*)

lined with railway sleepers. At some point after the war, the sleepers had been removed and without their support the ground, mainly chalk, slowly crumbled away. Apparently, the Orderly Sergeant was walking across the ground when a hole some 20 feet across and 10 feet deep suddenly opened up in front of him.

There was further correspondence between the Treasury and the Air Ministry in November, with the former claiming that RAF Manston was too big to justify its existence. The letter was written by a W. R. Fraser in the Treasury, and its content and the reply from the Air Ministry are worth quoting in full:

27 November 1924

S.6075.

Dear Cotton,

With reference to your letter of the 18th instant (East/8816) to Forsyth about Manston, the justification for this large place containing 'land enough for two aerodromes' is very difficult to find.

In order that we may be better able to follow it, may I trouble you with some further questions? If we have answers to them it will save trouble in the long run.

About £900,000 was spent on works and buildings there in the war period. You will no doubt agree that this expenditure, having regard to the circumstances in which it was incurred, is not a true criterion of the present value. Can you tell me (only rough figures needed):

(1) What the buildings are and for what air purpose they are adapted;

(2) What condition they are in, what is their annual cost of upkeep and what is to be needed for future adaptations;

(3) Whether there are now any ordinary dwelling houses (and if so how many) on the estate. (I gather a lot of land was parcelled into building sites but I am not clear whether any houses were built and if so whether they have been all pulled down);

(4) How many acres the 200 unbought plots represent;

(5) How the land is at present held (i.e. are you paying rent for what you have not bought and if so how much?);

(6) Whether by 'landing ground' at the end of your note you mean a ground for civil aviation or not.

Yours sincerely,

W. R. Fraser.

East 8/8816/F.W.

Air Ministry
Adastral House
Kingsway W.C.2
December 1924

Dear Fraser,

The following are the answers to the questions raised in your letter of the 27th ultimo (S.6075):

(1) The accommodation, which consists of hangars, workshops and other technical buildings, and living quarters, is under present policy, utilised for

(a) School of Technical Training (Men)
(b) One twin-engine bomber squadron.
(c) One Army Co-operation squadron.

(2) The buildings generally are of sound construction and in good condition. A few timber huts which have been converted into temporary married quarters for warrant officers and airmen are in fair condition only.

The average annual cost of maintenance of buildings is £5,000 and of roads £750.

No proposals have been formulated for future adaptations.

(3) No buildings of any description have been erected on any of the plots on the three estates when the Crown took possession.

(4) About 29 acres.

(5) Under D.O.R.A. [Defence of the Realm Act] the War Compensation Court has ruled that the owners of the plots are not entitled to any compensation in respect of the Crown occupation.

(6) No. We meant a landing ground for the Royal Air Force.

The correspondence was just part of the administrative game of 'ping pong' that went on for many years between the Treasury and Air Ministry. The Treasury for its part seems ill-informed in suggesting that Manston was being maintained for the use of civil aviation. It is evident that the Air Ministry was repeatedly having to justify the role of RAF Manston to the Treasury, and there was some expansion of the units based there.

In January 1925, the second Flight of No. 9 Squadron was formed and the establishment was raised again to include one wing commander, two squadron leaders, four flight lieutenants and eighteen flying officers. In the same month, Squadron Leader William James Yule Guilfoyle OBE, MC was posted in to Manston, and within a short while he was to take command of No. 9 Squadron from Daly.

Guilfoyle was another veteran of the First World War, having begun his service life as an officer with the 4th Light Horse Cavalry before joining the Royal Field Artillery. He had been seconded to the RFC in July 1915. He had then become a Flight Commander on No. 1 Squadron, Australian Flying Corps, and his first command had been that of No. 53 (Training) Squadron, before going on to command Nos 28 and 208 Squadrons, the latter having been equipped with Bristol Fighters at Ismailia in Egypt. After returning to the Home Establishment in March 1919, in August he was awarded a permanent commission with the rank of Major. He went on to command No. 113 Squadron, and No. 208 Squadron for the second time, and in 1922 took up the post of Commanding Officer of the School of Photography, before taking over No. 9 Squadron at Manston.

Also in January 1925, there was a change of command at Manston when Group Captain Godman took up the post of Deputy Director of Manning in the Air Ministry. He was succeeded as the Commanding Officer of Manston by Group Captain Sacheverell Arthur Hebden, who had returned to the Home Establishment after serving overseas in Iraq and had been promoted from Wing Commander on 1 January. Another 100 airmen were attached in to the School of Technical Training to train as drivers in the Armoured Car Unit as the role of the RAF was expanded to help the Army in Iraq.

Number 2 Squadron underwent a change of command in March 1925 when Squadron Leader Forbes handed over to Squadron Leader Richard Ernest Saul, who had returned to the Home Establishment after serving for four years in Iraq. Saul had previously commanded another unit that had been equipped with Bristol Fighters, having been the CO of No. 12 Squadron between 1919 and 1921, which had been based at Bickendorf in Germany. Saul would have fitted in well with Manston's sporting tradition, having played rugby for the RAF, and in the future was to excel in playing tennis for the service.

During the early months of 1925, No. 9 Squadron had begun to practise bombing and night-flying training, and in April it received its first Vickers Virginia, a new type of aircraft that was soon to replace the Vimy. The first Virginia, which had flown in November 1922, was little more than a modified version of the Vimy, but it was extensively modified through Mks 1, 2, and 3. It was powered by two 580 hp Napier Lion engines that gave it a top speed of 100 mph, and was capable of carrying a 3,000 lb bomb load.

It had been recognised early on that there were a number of issues concerning the stability and control of the Virginia, and it was not long before No. 9 Squadron, which was the first unit to receive the type, had its first serious accident. The incident, which occurred on 8 April 1925, even made the news in the national press and was mentioned in *The Times* with the headline 'Aeroplane Falls Into The Sea. Two Men Missing'.

There are few details of the accidents in the squadron's records, which just state: 'Virginia J7439 crashed into the sea near Birchington. Pilot F/O Bushell.

Two killed and two injured.' The accident happened at approximately 11.15 a.m., after J7439 had flown low over Birchington before crashing into the sea approximately a quarter of a mile off the coast. A number of local people had seen or heard the aircraft pass over the town, including Billy James who was employed as a waiter at the Beresford Hotel. When he heard a loud noise a few moments later he presumed that the aircraft had crashed into the sea. Together with a local doctor by the name of Flood, James made an outstanding effort to reach it.

There were four airmen on board the aircraft, and Pilot Officer Bushell was one of those who managed to scramble on top of the machine. He later claimed that he had also helped to rescue Aircraftman Mills from the water. He also remembered seeing the other officer and crew member, Pilot Officer Walker, climb on top of the machine out of the water as well, but then Bushell suddenly blacked out and the other two men were gone when he recovered. He was not sure what had happened to them, but suspected that they might have decided to try and swim towards the shore or, like himself, they had fallen unconscious and slipped from the wreckage.

At the time of the accident the visibility locally was very poor and a thick mist was hanging over the water, so some of those who had waded in to try and help soon found themselves lost or disorientated several hundred feet out to sea. Despite being somewhat handicapped by the fact that they were fully clothed, both Billy James and Dr Flood persisted with their rescue attempt and eventually, when they were approximately a quarter of a mile out, they sighted the aircraft and two airmen who were shouting for help. As James and the doctor approached the aircraft, they encountered a very strong current, so strong that they realised the only sensible thing to do was to go back and get more help. By that time a number of small boats had been launched and within a short while the rescue attempt was being properly organised and co-ordinated.

One of those who went to help was Ashley Milton, also employed at the Beresford Hotel. He had been walking along the seafront when he heard the sound of the aircraft crashing. With the air being still, the noise was so loud that he had at first been convinced that the aircraft had crashed into the cliffs. He waded out to sea, but could not see anything because of the mist. He repeatedly shouted, 'Are you safe?' and soon heard someone shouting 'No' on several occasions, but still unable to see anything, he waded back to the shore again. There he met a man called Burges and together they got on a motorcycle and rode off to another bay where they put out to sea in a boat. At the same time a number of other people were getting into boats and joining in the search, and very soon Bushell was found clinging on to the wreckage of the aircraft and was taken ashore. Soon afterwards, Aircraftman Grellis, described as a mechanic, was also found in the water close to the wreckage and was taken ashore in a boat.

Bushell had received only slight injuries to his head and legs, and was well enough to be taken back to the airfield at Manston where he was able to report what had happened. Grellis had sustained more serious injuries and was initially taken to the Beresford Hotel where he received some basic first aid before being taken to Ramsgate Hospital where he was admitted.

In the aftermath of the incident, motor boats from Margate cruised around the scene in the hope of finding the other two airmen around the wreckage of the Virginia, and later in the afternoon it was towed ashore into Beresford Gap. A look-out was posted on the top of the cliffs to maintain a watch in case either of the other two airmen should appear. The aircraft was examined by a team of mechanics from Manston and as far as could be discovered at the time, it was thought that the accident had been caused by a failure of the starboard engine. The bodies of the two other crew members, Pilot Officer Neil Walker from Lee-on-Solent and Aircraftman E. E. Mills, were never found. Walker, who had been posted to Manston straight out of training, had been at RAF Manston just two days.

Virginia J7439 was a Mk V, which was the first real production version that was different from earlier types because it was fitted with a third fin unit in the centre of the tail. Twenty-two Mk Vs were built out of a total of 124 Virginias produced, and J7439 was just one of many that were destroyed in accidents. There are various sets of figures accounting for the number of Virginias lost in accidents, and one of them states that it was eighty-one. If that figure is correct, it equates to 65 per cent being lost in accidents. Although J7439 was the first to be lost by No. 9 Squadron, it would not be the last.

It was the usual practice during this period for RAF fighter units to be sent away to summer camps where they underwent annual exercises at airfields other than those where they were based. Each squadron was sent to work with those elements of the military which were appropriate to their role, and in the case of Army Co-operation units it was with the Army. In 1925, No. 2 Squadron was sent to Okehampton in Devon for its summer camp, but at that time it was not an airfield but an Army station called Okehampton Camp. Nestling on the edge of Dartmoor, the camp had been built in 1893 especially for artillery training.

Three years later, in 1928, Okehampton would become an RAF station known as Folly Gate, but in 1925, the Army Co-operation units such as No. 2 Squadron operated from a strip of land beside the Army camp. The exercises at Okehampton were what were later termed an 'armament camp' and gave both the Army and Air Force crews the opportunity to work together, hence No. 2 Squadron's title as an Army Co-operation unit. Such exercises involved live firing and gave the Army gunners experience of firing against a moving target, while the air crews gained experience of bombing and the air gunners got an opportunity to practise their skills.

While No. 2 Squadron was away at its summer camp, No. 9 Squadron had Manston all to itself, undertaking an exercise concerning the fuel endurance and range of the Vickers Virginia. Two aircraft took part in the exercise, one of which flew for ten hours and ten minutes, and the other for nine hours and ten minutes. In August, the unit flew to the birthplace of naval aviation at Eastchurch, where it carried out its annual bombing practice.

The endurance and long-distance exercises continued on No. 9 Squadron into September, and at 2.35 a.m. on the 24th, the first aircraft took off from Manston to fly to Leuchars in Scotland, with four others following at 5-minute intervals. They all landed safely at Leuchars between 9.20 and 9.40 and were refuelled, taking on a total of 1,625 gallons together with the requisite amounts of oil for the engines. All five machines then left Leuchars together at 1 p.m. and landed back at Manston at 3.20. This was seen as a significant achievement, and within a few days No. 9 Squadron received a letter of congratulations from the Air Council. With the squadron having successfully accepted the Virginia into operational service, its predecessor, the Vimy, was phased out, the last one departing from Manston the following month.

There was a fire in the Officers' Mess in September which caused considerable damage to various parts of the building, but fortunately the worst of it was restricted to the Annexe. Because of budget cuts and financial restraints, it would be several years before the building was restored to its former glory.

In October, the School of Technical Training underwent its annual inspection, which was carried out by the AOC Inland Area, Air Vice-Marshal Tom Ince Webb-Bowen, who had taken over the post in March 1924. Webb-Bowen was an officer with a vast amount of experience, who had joined the Army in 1899. He had served with the Middlesex Regiment (Duke of Cambridge's Own) and the Bedfordshire Regiment, and had later become the Adjutant of the Madras Volunteer Corps. In 1912, after becoming disillusioned with the Army, he had re-mustered to the RFC and in July that year had learned to fly, being awarded the Royal Aero Club Certificate No. 242. Before being appointed as AOC Inland Area in March 1924, he had already held the post of AOC India and AOC No. 3 Group.

As well as inspecting the School of Technical Training at Manston, the AOC also showed an interest in No. 2 Squadron, probably because he had commanded that unit in March 1915 when it had been based on the Western Front. In fact, it had been his first command before returning to the Home Establishment to take up a post as an instructor. During his visit, Webb-Bowen was informed that in 1925, 266 pupils would pass out of the School of Technical Training, and that it was so busy that civilian clerks had had to be employed to relieve the burden on service personnel.

Oxford University Air Squadron (also known as the Varsity Squadron) was the second University Air Squadron to be formed and, on 11 October 1925, it was established with its HQ in Manor Road, Oxford. The Commanding Officer was Wing Commander Humphrey Rivas Raikes, originally from Sevenoaks, who was the Sub Rector at Exeter College. The third son of Canon William Allan Raikes from Goudhurst in Kent, he had only recently returned from South Africa where he had been the Principal of Witwatersrand University in Johannesburg.

Squadron Leader A. G. Weir, who was appointed as the Chief Flying Instructor, had been promoted to the rank of Flight Lieutenant in April 1920. Students were charged only £1 to join the squadron, but instruction was limited to lectures during term time. They were only given actual flying experience during the long breaks over the summer camps, and for the first five years of its existence they were to be held at Manston.

As well as the Vickers Virginias, No. 9 Squadron also operated a number of smaller aircraft. On its establishment were a number of Avro 504Ks that were used for training its pilots and those of the University Air Squadron. Some of them, such as E3798, had arrived on the unit earlier that year in March, while others, such as E2914, were not taken on charge at Manston until November. On 16 December, these two aircraft collided over the airfield at 700 feet, resulting in the death of one airman and the loss of both Avros. Leading Aircraftman Dunn was the pilot killed, while Leading Aircraftman Parrish escaped serious injury after descending by parachute.

CHAPTER 11

The Second Decade

At the beginning of 1926 there were various changes to the administrative organisation at Manston and a Civil Assistant Adjutant was appointed, with Flight Lieutenant Fenn taking over that role. Flight Lieutenant Cuckney DSO relieved Flight Lieutenant Fuller of his duties and role of Adjutant, as the latter was being transferred to the Reserve.

In early 1926, Wing Commander Vivian Gaskell-Blackburn DSC, AFC, who had recently been promoted from Squadron Leader, arrived at Manston as the Deputy Commanding Officer of No. 9 Squadron. He officially took over on 28 February, but as was usual, practised with Squadron Leader Guilfoyle as Vice-OC and took full command the following month. Guilfoyle was appointed as a staff officer in the Wessex Bombing Area.

The following month, RAF Manston was transferred from No. 1 Group to No. 23 Group, which was under the command of Air Commodore Ian Malcolm Bonham-Carter CB, OBE. Number 1 Group, originally formed in April 1918, had undergone several changes, being retitled the South-Eastern Area Group, Southern Area Group, and in April 1920, Inland Area Group. In April 1926, it was to disappear from the Order of Battle completely, being renumbered as No. 22 Group, and RAF Manston became part of No. 23 Group (Training) Inland Area, which was more fitting for its role.

Bonham-Carter was an officer with a vast amount of experience in the role of staff and command as his operational flying career had been cut short in 1914. While visiting his old regiment on the front line, the Northumberland Fusiliers, his aircraft had crashed and he had lost a leg as a result of the incident. He also had considerable experience of the role played by the School of Technical Training, having been Commandant of the unit in 1917, when it was based at Halton. Prior to taking over No. 23 Group, Bonham-Carter had also commanded, among others, No. 11 Group (Irish) and No. 3 Group in October 1925. He had taken up his appointment as AOC No. 23 Group on 1 April 1926. During the time that he commanded No. 23 Group he had an

Avro 504 specially adapted for his disability so that he could continue to get around to the stations under his command.

Overall, 1926 was not a very exciting or distinguished year at Manston, apart from the fact that the station celebrated its first ten years of service. It was, however, the year of the General Strike and, as usual on such occasions, the RAF was called in to help out. When the strike was called on 4 May, No. 9 Squadron was transferred to Biggin Hill and given the job of delivering the newspaper *The British Gazette* to Catterick. At Manston the period of the strike was known as the 'crisis period' and, in typical RAF fashion, a 'crisis organisation' was established and an officer appointed as the 'Crisis Officer'. That role was given to Flying Officer H. A. Haines DFC, and one of the things that he had to do was to organise a party of officers and airmen who were dispatched to the No. 1 Stores Depot at RAF Kidbrooke on 1 May, under the command of Squadron Leader Arthur Harold Measures OBE. A further party of ten officers and thirty-one airmen followed them to Kidbrooke on the 11th, but by that time the strike was nearly over and within two days it was called off.

During the period of the conflict, No. 9 Squadron's Virginias carried a total of 17 tons 87 lb of newspapers and freight. The aircraft completed seventy-one flights, covering a distance comparable to 12,220 miles, and that amounted to a flying time of 362 hours and 35 minutes. Measures and his party returned to Manston on the 16th, but the official signal from HQ Inland Area announcing 'Crisis ends' did not arrive at Manston until the 18th.

In June, No. 9 Squadron was transferred under the command of the Wessex Bombing Area and on 3 July, its Virginias took part in the Long Range Reliability Trials for twin-engine bombing aircraft. That also included an appearance and display at RAF Hendon.

The Oxford University Air Squadron was attached to RAF Manston in July for its first summer camp, which ran from the 6th to the 21st on what was called a Practice Flight School. Students were given tuition in Avro 504Ks fitted with 80 hp Gnome Lambda rotary engines that ran on castor oil and gave off noxious fumes, which made a number of student pilots feel quite sick. The twenty-officers who took part in the camp were accommodated in the Officers' Mess. They flew from 6 a.m. until 1 p.m. and then took part in various sporting events until taking dinner in the evening.

Their experience was not confined solely to the Avros. The students also flew with the resident squadrons at Manston. It was claimed that while taking part in No. 9 Squadron's Virginias sorties on night-flying exercises, they found that the rear turret made an excellent bed. With No. 2 Squadron in their Bristol Fighters they took part in photo-reconnaissance sorties, and it is said that they were amazed at the quality of the photos they had taken of the local resorts. The students were inspected during their stay by Air Marshal Sir

John Maitland Salmond, who was impressed by their knowledge and turnout. Altogether the University Air Squadron students completed 205 hours' flying time, and the summer camp was considered to be a huge success.

On the same day that the Oxford University Air Squadron had arrived at Manston, the Secretary of the Air Council wrote to the Treasury on behalf of its President. The letter concerned the fact that it had been found necessary for more land to be requisitioned, especially the site of the railway that ran from the aerodrome to what was now the Southern Railway at Birchington. It was stated that the whole of the land required for the aerodrome had already been acquired by the Air Council apart from 138 small plots that were coloured blue, green and pink on the plans. Despite every effort having been made to trace the owners of those plots, very few of them had been found, and it had been impossible to agree terms with those who had been contacted. As a result, it had been found necessary to invoke the compulsory powers vested in the Department by the Defence Act of 1842. The necessary certificates of ownership had been executed by the Lord Lieutenant of the County of Kent and an engrossment of the Treasury Warrant. This was needed before the Department could proceed with the acquisitions and it required the signatures of two members of the House of Lords. It was requested that this should be done as soon as possible and the documents returned to the Secretary of the Air Council.

After all that had taken place, and with more land having been acquired, it might have seemed that the future of RAF Manston was secure, but that was far from the case. In a letter from the Treasury to the Air Council, dated 14 July 1926, it was suggested that after further consideration, it might find it practicable to re-sell or let such portions of land that were not required for flying purposes. It was pointed out that the Air Ministry had stated that because the purchase of the whole of the land comprising the aerodrome had not been completed, it was not possible to supply the information needed by their Lordships. The 'game' between the Air Ministry and the Treasury was not yet over!

On Monday 24 July, an Avro 504 belonging to No. 9 Squadron crashed close to Chapel Hill in Ramsgate, but the pilot, Leading Aircraftman Parrish, baled out and escaped with only light injuries and bruising. Although the squadron was mainly equipped with the Virginia bomber, the Avros were used as 'hacks' and for training purposes. Parrish was on a training flight when the controls jammed as it was flying over the airfield, and there are few details of the incident except for those reported in the press. The *Western Argus* published a brief account of the incident on Tuesday 3 August and it claimed that on the day of the accident thousands of holidaymakers in Ramsgate experienced a thrill when an aircraft reportedly flying at 5,000 feet went out of control. The pilot was seen to walk out on to the wing before jumping off and very slowly parachuting to earth. It claimed that it took him twenty minutes to gain land and that he suffered only a few cuts and light bruising. The aircraft was reported as crashing 2 miles away, but there was no mention of place, type of aircraft, or the unit it belonged to. The *Isle of Thanet Gazette* published a similar account, but differed in that it claimed that the cause of the accident was engine failure.

In September, the station was inspected by the AOC Inland Area, Air Vice-Marshal Webb-Bowen, who was making his second inspection since he had taken office. The following month, the Chaplain at Manston, the Revd R. E. V. (Group Captain) Benson was appointed as the Chaplain in Chief of the RAF. He was replaced by the Revd K. C. Warner, and although the Revd Benson was sorry to leave Manston, his appointment was a great honour for both him and the station.

There was further correspondence during September between the Air Ministry and the Treasury about the future of RAF Manston, and in a letter dated the 6th it was suggested that the station could be closed or reduced to the status of an emergency landing ground:

Dear Fass,

Your official letter of 14th July, 1926, (S.6075) about land at Manston.

I am sorry to say that we are still not in a position to give a definite answer to your enquiries, as the future of this station remains very uncertain.

As Cotton told Forsyth in November, 1924, the scheme was then to move the School of Technical Training (Men) from Manston to Cranwell, when the Boys' Wing went to Halton, to continue to use Manston for Home Defence Squadrons until the expansion scheme was complete, and after that to keep it as a landing ground.

The Boys' Wing has now left Cranwell for Halton, and we propose to move the School from Manston to Cranwell in the near future. We referred officially to this transfer in our letter 627634/25 (F.W.) dated 10th May 1926, (your reference S.28817) and you will be receiving a further official letter on the subject soon.

A short time ago it was thought that after this move Manston might be surrendered entirely but now there is little doubt that it will be necessary to retain the aerodrome as an emergency landing ground.

Manston had started off as an emergency landing ground in 1916, and ten years later it looked like it would return to that role. There were obviously a lot of things going on behind the scenes that were not recorded and are not in the official records. The School of Technical Training remained at

Manston for many more years and, for some reason, was retained for the use of operational units.

The Isle of Thanet had a royal visitor on 24 November, when HRH the Prince of Wales arrived in the area and was met by the Station Commander, Group Captain Hebden, who was accompanied by the Mayor of Ramsgate. They met the Prince at an official reception in Ramsgate and the route was lined by personnel from Manston under the command of Squadron Leader Measures. RAF Manston also provided a guard of honour and No. 9 Squadron's Virginias supplied an escort for the Prince during his visit.

Number 9 Squadron underwent its annual inspection during November by the AOC Wessex Bombing Area, a former naval officer, Air Vice-Marshal Sir John Miles Steel. He had learned to fly in March 1918 and had been awarded Royal Aero Club Certificate No. 5731. No. 9 Squadron also had a change of command at this time. Wing Commander C. C. Durston took over with effect from 29 December, when Gaskell-Blackburn was posted to the Depot at Uxbridge. Durston, who was a former Commanding Officer of No. 15 Squadron, had attended the School of Army Co-operation at Old Sarum. He was posted in to Manston from No. 21 Group (Training) HQ at West Drayton where he had served on the staff.

At the end of 1926, the total number of movements of airmen who had been posted in and out of Manston, exclusive of attachments or reservists, was 1,560. The number of airmen who had passed out of the School of Technical Training in 1926 was 488, which was 222 more than the previous year and a growth of almost 80 per cent.

Among the School's headquarters staff in December 1926 were Group Captain Hebden (Commanding Officer), Squadron Leader Stewart (Administrative), Flight Lieutenant Bartlett (Adjutant), and Flight Lieutenant C. Fenn (Civilian Assistant Adjutant). The Stores Officers were Flight Lieutenants H. H. Ridridge and H. V. Robins. The Officer in Command of the Practice Flight of the School was Flying Officer H. A. Haines. Squadron Leader Measures was the Officer in Command of Training Headquarters, and there were another four officers of the rank of Flight Lieutenant and another three Flying Officers with various responsibilities.

CHAPTER 12

Slow Boat to China

The year 1927 did not get off to a good start for No. 9 Squadron. On 11 January, Vickers Virginia J7435, flown by Sergeant Richardson, landed in Holland after getting lost during a flight from Spittlegate in Lincolnshire to Manston. Flying above the clouds, the pilot made a huge navigational error, crossing the North Sea and finally landing at Oosterhout. An officer from the Air Defence of Great Britain was sent to Holland to investigate the incident, and the aircraft was eventually returned to Manston.

In March, another Virginia, J7425, piloted by Flying Officer Barlow, force landed in the Thames Estuary after both of the aircraft's engines failed. The incident happened at approximately 9 p.m. and although every effort was made by the four men on board to attract attention, help did not arrive for a long time. They fired a number of flares from the Verey pistol, but despite that and continuously shouting very loudly for help, it was six hours before they were rescued.

The downed aircraft was eventually spotted and its crew picked up by the trawler SS *Pickmere*, but because the vessel did not carry a radio they were unable to notify the authorities of what had happened until they were landed in Sheerness at midday. Amazingly, the Virginia had continued to float, even with the four airmen sitting on top of it, and the trawler was able to tow it in. During the subsequent investigation it was found that the cause of the crash was pilot error and that one of the crew had inadvertently switched off two of the aircraft's main petrol cocks.

There was sporting success for RAF Manston when the station won the RAF's Cross Country Championship held at South Farnborough on 16 March. Aircraftman F. W. Turner of RAF Uxbridge won the individual event and was the sole survivor of a very successful Uxbridge team that had recently been broken up. A number of members of that team had been posted to Manston and there were murmurs of discontent, complaining that these postings were the reason for Manston's success.

In the spring of 1927, No. 2 Squadron was ordered to prepare immediately for a move overseas, to the distant shores of China, where it was to assist the Shanghai Defence Force that had been raised in London on 22 January. Because of conflict between Nationalist and Communist forces, angry armed Chinese mobs had threatened British concessions such as the city and port of Hankow, where British residents had been forced to take shelter on a Royal Navy cruiser. Concern about British and European residents in Shanghai forced the Government to commit forces to protect them, and the main element of the ground force was the Queen's Royal Regiment. It had set sail from Southampton in January, and No. 2 Squadron in its role as an Army Co-operation unit was sent out to support it.

The movement orders arrived at Manston at 11 a.m. on 8 April, and the squadron was informed that it would also sail from Southampton on the 20th, so the frantic efforts of packing up and sorting things out began straightaway. The following day, the first five Bristol Fighters were flown to Farnborough where they were stripped down to be packed away in large wooden crates at RAF Ascot, which had been used as an aircraft park during the First World War. Pilot Officers Stokes and Mathews stayed behind to supervise the process while the other pilots were flown back to Manston by No. 9 Squadron in the Virginias.

On the 10th, the four remaining Bristol Fighters of No. 2 Squadron were flown to Farnborough by Flight Lieutenant Bain, Flying Officer Hadden, and Pilot Officers F. L. Wilson and H. G. S. Wilson. The unit also had to be brought up to its establishment, so the following day Flight Lieutenant Lock and Flying Officer Tighe were posted in from No. 12 Squadron at Andover. Two days later, Lock was sent to the Air Ministry in London to collect maps of China and to be briefed and updated on a new grid system that was to be used. Both airmen and officers over the next few days were involved in packing and being issued and fitted out with their tropical kits.

With only a few days to organise the supply of tropical issue shorts and shirts, there would have been little time for measuring up and the uniforms were probably even more ill-fitting than that which was the norm! Orders were received for the squadron to leave Birchington station at 4.30 a.m., whence they would be taken to Southampton to embark on the steamship HMT *Neuralia*. The troopship was an old coal-burning vessel that had been launched in Glasgow in 1912. Working for the British India Steam Navigation Company, it was a regular on the voyage to China and the Far East. Wing Commander Primrose, who had returned from Iraq where he had been involved with the Armoured Car Detail and was now a Staff Officer at the Directorate of Equipment, visited the squadron just before it was due to leave to say his 'farewells', wishing both the officers and airmen well on their long voyage to the East.

A flight of Bristol Fighters from No. 2 Squadron over the airfield. The photograph was probably taken in April or May 1927, before the final move to China. (*John Williams*)

Not everything or everyone was travelling from Southampton, and a convoy made up of transport from No. 2 Squadron was ordered to drive to Birkenhead for embarkation on the steamship SS *Sarpedon*. Launched in 1923, the 11,321-ton ship of the Blue Funnel Line was capable of just 17 knots. On the 14th, four lorries, four Crossley tenders and three trailers arrived at Manston to transport the squadron's stores on the 300-mile journey north. The transport party, under the supervision of Flying Officer Anderson and Pilot Officer Stokes, departed from Manston at 8 a.m. It had been arranged that the main transport and stores should be loaded on to the *Sarpedon* on the 23rd, while all the ammunition was to be loaded on to the *City of Poona* on the 25th.

At 2.15 a.m. on the 20th, the officers and airmen of No. 2 Squadron marched down the road to Birchington railway station and two-and-a-quarter hours later, the train left on its journey to Southampton. It arrived at 10.30, and before they boarded the *Neuralia* the squadron was inspected by the AOC Inland Area, Sir Charles Alexander Holcombe Longcroft CB, CMG, DSO, AFC, a veteran of the Welsh Regiment who had joined the RFC in April 1912, after he had been seconded to the Air Battalion. One of his most notable achievements had been in August 1913, when he had flown Lieutenant-Colonel Sykes to Montrose, completing the RFC's longest flight in a time of 7 hours and 20 minutes.

Although not directly concerned with RAF Manston, No. 2 Squadron was one of the units with long-term connections to the station, and it is worth recording its activities in the Far East, particularly because it was destined to return to Manston just a few months after it had departed.

The first port of call on the way was Malta, where the ship arrived a week later, on the 27th. By that time, the airmen would have discovered that life on board ship was not exactly what they might have imagined. Airmen, like soldiers, were given a specific space to live in, which in most cases was quite limited, so their bed was a hammock which had to be rigged up in their sleeping quarters. They were also likely to be given tasks on board ship such as sentry duties and galley duties which often meant, among other things, peeling large amounts of potatoes. There were also general cleaning duties, and the ship had to be prepared for inspection by the Captain at 11 a.m. every day.

From Malta the *Neuralia* sailed to Port Said, where it arrived at 4 p.m. on the 30th. While No. 2 Squadron was there, it carried out a route march to exercise the men. This was standard practice at most ports of call to get the men back into shape and exercise their limbs, which in most cases had been rested for extended periods. The *Neuralia* then set sail for Colombo in Ceylon (Sri Lanka) where it arrived on 12 May and the airmen underwent another route march with Flight Lieutenants Bain and Simpson in command. From there the ship sailed to Singapore, arriving on 18 May, and then continuing to Hong Kong where the squadron stayed for three days before proceeding to Shanghai.

The squadron began unloading its transport and stores on 1 June, some six weeks after marching out of Manston, and on the same day the first four Bristol Fighters were put ashore in crates. The four aircraft belonged to 'B' Flight, which began to assemble them the following day, while Wing Commander Barratt went to Tientsin to assess the possibility of setting up an aerodrome there. Sanitary conditions were so bad that the squadron appointed Flying Officer Walker as the 'Sanitary Officer', and health issues were to plague the unit.

On 7 June, the strength of the unit was noted as being 33 officers and 205 airmen, but those figures were to vary as the number of those reporting sick increased. Aircraftman 2nd Class Taylor (505516) was the first casualty, being admitted to No. 12 Field Ambulance Station on the same day. The first flights also took place on the 7th, and Bristol Fighters J6735, J7652 and J7651 were test flown by Flying Officer Moreton, while J7768 was tested by Squadron Leader Lowry.

The officers took over the clubhouse of the Shanghai Race Club for their mess and the airmen took over a shop opposite the Star Garage for use as their billet. Six Chinese sweepers were employed for sanitary duties on a wage of $13 a month, but that seems to have had little impact in preventing further cases of sickness. Corporal Clarke reported sick on the 16th and was admitted to No. 2 General Hospital, which reduced the strength of No. 2 Squadron to 203. He was soon followed by Leading Aircraftman Hurst, who was admitted to the Royal Hospital.

Flying Officer Moreton, flying with Leading Aircraftman Rendle as his passenger, flew the first sortie in China on the 17th, taking seven mosaic plates of land after a run over a nearby canal. Over the following week, Moreton flew several more sorties with a variety of passengers, and several other pilots began to fly operational photo-reconnaissance missions.

Towards the end of June, the situation regarding those reporting sick was getting out of hand. Although Hurst was discharged from hospital, Aircraftman 2nd Class Hart was admitted. On the 29th, both Corporal Stratham and Leading Aircraftman Wilkin were admitted to No. 7 General Hospital, followed the next day by Leading Aircraftman Toms. It was a similar story for the next week, with a number of other airmen being admitted to hospital, while on the 13th, Hart died at No. 7 General Hospital. It was noted in the squadron records that he had previously been burnt, but there is no mention of the actual cause of death.

On 20 July, a number of successful sorties were flown in order to take photos of the area between the international race course, the Wang Poo and Woosung arsenal. It must have been a relief, however, when orders were received on the same day for No. 2 Squadron to return to the UK, its personnel embarking on the SS *Nivara* and SS *Divanha* on 6 and 13 September respectively. The *Nivara* was a 9,071-ton vessel built in Glasgow in 1913 for the British India Steam Navigation Company and was capable of just 14 knots; the *Divanha* was an 8,092-ton ship built in 1905 for the P&O Line. Not only was the squadron to return to the UK, but to Manston, and although many members of the unit must have been delighted, their return was later marred by a series of bad accidents.

CHAPTER 13

The Future of Manston

From 17-19 May 1927, RAF Manston underwent its annual inspection by the AOC No. 23 Group, Air Vice-Marshal Bonham-Carter. In June, there was further correspondence between the Air Ministry and the Treasury regarding the future of the station. It is interesting that the term 'semi-official correspondence' was used in the first paragraph of a letter sent to the Treasury. It is not known whether that implied that previous letters from the Treasury had been of a personal nature and not necessarily the views of the Air Council or the Government:

704384/26 (F.W.)

14th June 1927

Sir,

    With reference to the last paragraph of your letter dated 14th July 1926, and subsequent semi-official correspondence relative to the acquisition of land at Manston. I am commanded by the Air Council to acquaint you, for the information of the Lords Commissioners of His Majesty's Treasury, that the total sum expended up to the present, including interest on purchase money, surveyor's cost and solicitors' fees, is £29,265, and it is estimated that the further sum payable in respect of the 138 small plots to be acquired by compulsory powers will be £2,700.

    With regard to the question of the disposal of part of the land, I am to request you to inform Their Lordships that it will not be possible for some years to relinquish any portion of the station. The Council are at present considering the practicability of transferring to Cranwell the Electrical and Wireless School (now at Flowerdown) instead of the School of Technical Training, and it is probable that the latter will remain at Manston indefinitely. The station will also be occupied for some years at least by an Army Co-operation Squadron and by one Bombing Squadron of the Home

Defence Force for which no other accommodation will be available.

As soon as the development of the Home Defence Force scheme makes it possible to settle the permanent complement of Manston and to transfer any units not included therein, the whole question will be further reviewed.

This is the last letter that is available in the archives concerning the development of RAF Manston during the period when its future was open to debate. As stated in the letter, the School of Technical Training was to remain at Manston and, although not indefinitely, certainly for many more years in the future. An Army Co-operation unit in the form of No. 2 Squadron was also to remain at Manston for several more years, as were other operational units, making the future of the station more secure.

The Oxford University Air Squadron returned to Manston in July for its second summer camp and each student was allocated 1 per cent of the total flying hours that it was allowed with the Practice Flight. Membership of the squadron had risen to seventy-five, and a small number of students had gained unofficial flying experience when an aeroplane had landed on Ferry Hinksey Road in Oxford and the pilot had begun to offer pleasure flights. The authorities quickly intervened, however, and undergraduates at Oxford were banned from flying in the machine.

As well as the practical flying experience at Manston there were lectures on rigging, engines, and airmanship. Five junior officers were attached to Manston's Practice Flight and came from a number of different fighter and bomber squadrons: Flying Officer B. N. T. Hare from No. 43(F) Squadron based at Tangmere; Flying Officer L. H. Newton from No. 3(F) Squadron at Upavon; Pilot Officer T. B. Fenwick from No. 11(B) Squadron at Netheravon; Pilot Officer H. H. Brooks from No. 58(B) Squadron at Worthy Down; and Pilot Officer J. G. D. Armour from the Central Flying School, then based at Wittering.

Students were also shown how to use a new piece of ground equipment that was in use at Manston called the 'Hucks starter', named after its inventor Captain Bentfield Charles Hucks, who had been attached to the Aircraft Manufacturing Company as the Chief Test Pilot. The 20 hp engine of Model T Ford had been adapted as the basis for the machine, which had been designed to swing the propeller on starting the engine. The device was fixed to the centre of the propeller to swing it and, when it began to turn, it automatically released itself from the propeller boss. It had been designed as early as 1916, but the death of thirty-four-year-old Hucks in November 1918 possibly delayed its development. There is no record of how safe it was to use, but it was almost certainly safer than the traditional manual method where airmen risked losing their heads.

During its time at Manston, the Oxford University Air Squadron was inspected by the Chief of the Air Staff, Sir Hugh Trenchard, on 11 July. He was accompanied by Air Vice-Marshal Sir Ivo Lucius Beresford Vesey. Trenchard had recently been promoted to Marshal of the Royal Air Force. Vesey was the Director of Organisation and Staff at the Air Ministry and his rank was only an honorary appointment, awarded in August 1923, when he had been seconded to the RAF. The following year he was returned to the establishment of the Army with the rank of Colonel. The Hon. M. C. H. Drummond also inspected the unit and then joined the party that went on to inspect the workshops of the School of Technical Training. The staff and airmen should have been in a good mood, as the School was about to close down for two weeks' summer leave from 22 July until 8 August.

There also were a number of changes to key positions at Manston at this time. Squadron Leader Henry Sam Francis Temple Jerrard was posted in as the Senior Stores Officer to replace Flight Lieutenant Eldridge, who was posted overseas.

By the end of the year, flying had become so popular amongst the Oxford OAS students that the squadron was provided with four Avro 504Ns, based at Upper Heyford. The fact that the squadron was given its own aeroplanes could possibly have made Manston a little superfluous, but that was not the case, and the station continued to have close contacts with the unit for many years.

To make up for the absence of No. 2 Squadron, a number of other units were attached to Manston, the first one being No. 605 (County of Warwick) Squadron, which arrived on 31 July. It was an Auxiliary Air Force day bomber squadron equipped with the DH.9A, the likes of which had not been seen regularly at Manston for many years. Under the command of Squadron Leader J. A. C. Wright, the unit was normally based at Castle Bromwich and usually recruited its personnel from the area around Birmingham. It was attached to Manston for fourteen days' annual training, associated with the Air Defence of Great Britain Command.

On 4 August, No. 605 Squadron lost an aircraft when one of its DH.9s, E8711, crashed while taking off from Manston and was completely burnt out. The aircraft had seen a considerable amount of service. It had first been taken on charge by No. 30 Squadron on 21 March 1923, but was sent to the Packing Depot at Ascot before being transported to India where it had served with that unit at Hinaida. It had been returned to the UK in April 1927, and was taken on charge by No. 605 Squadron on 23 May. There are no details of any casualties involved in this incident at Manston.

On 13 August, No. 13 (Army Co-operation) Squadron was attached to Manston from Andover under the Command of Squadron Leader G. R. A. Deacon. The unit, equipped with Bristol Fighters, would remain at Manston until early September, and during that time it would be begin to be equipped with the Armstrong Whitworth Atlas.

On 15 September, the Overseas Draft No. 1 was inspected by the AOC No. 23 Group, Air Vice-Marshal Bonham-Carter, and four days later it left Manston for Southampton, its port of embarkation, under the command of Flight Lieutenant Haines. According to RAF Manston's records, this was the first time that an overseas draft had proceeded directly from a unit to its port of embarkation, instead of the usual practice whereby they departed from the Depot at Uxbridge.

The first elements of No. 2 Squadron arrived back at RAF Manston on 23 October under the command of Flight Lieutenant Lock, the second detachment arriving three days later, with Commanding Officer Squadron Leader Frederick Sowrey. It was almost six months to the day since they had left the station, and most officers and airmen were certainly glad to be back.

At the end of October, three Japanese officers inspected RAF Manston and were escorted by Flight Lieutenant Philip Fletcher Fullard DSO, MC, AFC from the Staff Directorate and Operations Intelligence Department. Fullard was a veteran and ace pilot from the Great War who had been credited with forty-six kills, but had been overlooked and eclipsed by the achievements of other aces such as Albert Ball, Billy Bishop and James McCudden. He was another officer who was destined for air rank, and in the following years was to have further close connections with Manston. The names of the Japanese officers who visited Manston were noted as Commander Nagamins, Lieutenant Commander Nakamura and Lieutenant Muneyuri, but no details were recorded about the exact purpose of their visit.

A few days later, the station was inspected by the AOC Inland Area, Air Vice-Marshal Longcroft. In 1919, he had been appointed as the first Commandant of the RAF College at Cranwell, but more significantly had had close associations with No. 2 Squadron on which he had been a Flight Commander in 1912. Having inspected the squadron on the quayside at Southampton, he would no doubt have shown some interest in his former unit and in hearing of its exploits on the other side of the world.

On 31 December, it was recorded that the total number of movements of airmen in 1927, exclusive of attachments and reservists for training, was 1,791. There had been 97 discharges and transfers to the Reserve, and the number of pupils passing out of the School of Technical Training was 841.

Number 2 Overseas Draft departed from Manston at the end February 1928, and was closely followed a few days later by No. 3 Overseas Draft and an Armoured Car Crew Draft destined for Iraq. All three drafts departed from Southampton.

On Wednesday 14 March, two aircraft from the two resident squadrons at Manston were involved in a collision between a Bristol Fighter of No. 2 Squadron and a Vickers Virginia of No. 9 Squadron. The Virginia was one of five machines flying in formation over the airfield when, according to eyewitness accounts, a Bristol Fighter flying alone suddenly dived and collided with the Virginia. One of the wings of the Bristol Fighter immediately crumpled up and the aircraft fell 500 feet, landing near the hangars with its nose buried in the ground, totally wrecked.

Rescuers were on the scene very quickly, but both airmen, Flying Officer Horace J. J. Mumford-Mathews and his passenger Lieutenant David Francis Cumon Scott of the 1st Essex Regiment, were already dead by the time they arrived. Both officers were twenty-two years old, and it is understood that Scott was undergoing a training course with the Army Co-operation unit. Mumford-Mathews was a great sportsman and the holder of the RAF Welterweight Boxing Championship title, having beaten Pilot Officer Willis of Calshot in March 1927.

The Virginia being flown alone by Flying Officer Ratcliffe had its left wing badly damaged and the propellers of one of the engines were broken, but with remarkable skill he managed to get the aircraft on the ground without further damage. Ratcliffe landed approximately half a mile from the airfield on land that was part of Manston Court Farm belonging to a Mr Philpott. The two aircraft involved in the incident were Bristol Fighter J7666, which had been taken on charge by No. 2 Squadron on 10 July 1925, and Vickers Virginia J8239. The strange thing about this incident was that it was reported in *The Sydney Morning Herald* the following day, but as far as is known, neither Mumford-Mathews nor Scott had any connections with anyone in Australia!

Just a few days later, on the 17th, the air crew of No. 9 Squadron had to put the incident behind them when a flight of Virginias were detailed to fly up to Hendon to take part in an air display. There were royal guests at the air show, including King Amanullah of Afghanistan and his wife Queen Souriya, who were on a state visit to Britain as part of their European tour. While they were in the country, the royal visitors also toured the School of Technical Training (Boys) at Halton, and on the 21st were taken to Croydon Airport, where the king had his first ever flight in an Armstrong Whitworth Argosy. Since his arrival in Europe, the king had taken a keen interest in aviation, and after his flight over London was thrilled to visit the cockpit and have the controls and instruments explained to him.

Two days later, Squadron Leader Donald Lane Ingpen from the Legal Branch gave a series of lectures to the officers at Manston about air force law and King's Regulations. Ingpen was from the Air Force Department of the Office of the Judge Advocate General, and his promotion to Squadron Leader had been announced in the 1927 New Year's Honours List. With the exception of a small number of officers who had studied law, this may well have been one of the more boring aspects of their job. Officers, however, did not spend all their time flying, and as part of their role carrying out general duties there were many administrative tasks to be performed on a daily basis.

Squadron Leader Sowrey MC, DFC handed over command of No. 2

Squadron on 1 April, after leading the unit for over fifteen months and through some tough times in Ireland and China. His successor was Squadron Leader Harold Melsome Probyn, who was posted in from the Staff School of Army Co-operation at Old Sarum. He had previously served with No. 2 Squadron and, among other things, had had some strange experiences in the desert in Egypt, where he had been based at Ismailia.

On one occasion, while flying over the desert, he had to make a forced landing when his engine failed. Describing the incident in a lecture he gave to the Yeovil branch of the Royal Aeronautical Society, he said that while he was tinkering about and trying to repair the engine he dropped a bunch of keys and despite an extensive search, failed to find them. Just a short while later, Probyn had the same problem again, and was forced to make another unscheduled landing in the desert. As he jumped out of the aircraft and began examining the engine, something caught his eye. Looking down, he saw his bunch of keys right underneath his feet! It was pure coincidence, and he claimed that he must have landed in exactly the same spot as before. Even so, to find keys that so easily could have been buried under tons of the desert's shifting sand was nothing less than a miracle.

On 2 April, just a day after Probyn took over command, No. 2 Squadron lost another two airmen in a tragic accident that happened near Colchester in Bristol Fighter J7651, when Flying Officer Jack Hadden flew the aircraft into a tree. The aircraft had been carrying out a low-level strafing exercise with infantry as part of an Army Co-operation exercise with units from the 11th Brigade. The passenger was Aircraftman Towers from No. 2 Squadron.

Twenty-six-year-old Hadden was the youngest member of the family of the late Francis John Hadden and Marion Kate 'May' Thomas of Scarborough but originally from Ceylon. The family had already suffered more than their fair share of grief. His father, who was fifty-five years old, had served as a Lieutenant with the 42nd Remount Squadron of the Army Service Corps and had died of pneumonia in the Red Cross Hospital in Cairo.

The family had consisted of three sons, Arthur, Thomas Harvey and Jack, and a daughter, Freda, who was the eldest child. Jack, who had been seconded from the Black Watch Regiment, was the second of the sons to be killed. His older brother, twenty-three-year-old 2nd Lieutenant Arthur Hadden had been killed in Mesopotamia while serving with the 53rd Sikhs. Flying Officer Jack Hadden was not married, but just a few weeks before, on 22 March, it had been announced in *The Times* newspaper that he had been engaged to a Caroline Mary (Carol), the daughter of Charles Farquhar who was a retired member of the Indian Police Force.

A detachment from No. 25(F) Squadron arrived at Manston on 25 May to carry out exercises with No. 9 Squadron's Vickers Virginias. After being disbanded at Scopwick at the end of 1920, No. 25 Squadron had re-formed at Hawkinge and was equipped with the Gloster Grebe. Like a number of other units such as No. 2 Squadron, No. 25 Squadron had left its own base of Hawkinge and served for several months overseas, operating in Turkey. In 1922, it had returned to Hawkinge, an airfield not too distant from Manston, being situated to the west of Dover. It was to be the squadron's home base for several years.

In early July, No. 9 Squadron moved out to North Coates to take part in the annual arms practice camp and while it was away, the Oxford University Air Squadron held its third summer camp at Manston. On this occasion it consisted of three separate detachments of twenty-five students, the first ones arriving on 24 June and staying until 7 July. The following day the second batch arrived, and their camp lasted until 21 July. The third and final batch arrived on the 22nd and trained at Manston until 4 August.

The Practice Flight consisted of two DH.9As and seven Avro 621 Tutors, the successor to the Avro 504, described as 'Lynx Avros' because they were fitted with a 240 hp Armstrong Siddeley Lynx engine. Another DH.9A and two Tutors were also held in reserve for the Practice Flight.

The Chief Instructor of the University Air Squadron's Practice Flight was Wing Commander Alfred Guy Roland Garrod MC, DFC. He had been seconded to the RFC from the Warwick Yeomanry in 1913, and had been awarded the Military Cross in that year. He had also been mentioned in despatches three times. In 1919, after being awarded the DFC, he attended a course of instruction at the Royal Naval College, Greenwich, and served as an instructor at the RAF Staff College. In 1925, he had been awarded a permanent commission as a Squadron Leader and was appointed as the Commanding Officer of RAF North Coates.

His seven fellow instructors on the University Air Squadron came from a variety of different backgrounds and units. Flight Lieutenant J. J. Williams AFC, Flight Lieutenant T. B. Bruce, and Flying Officer H. M. Schofield came from the Station Flight at Upper Heyford, while Flying Officers C. Clarkson and J. G. D. Armour were from the Central Flying School. Flying Officers B. C. Mason and R. F. P. Pope had been seconded from No. 3 Flying Training School.

As was the normal practice while the University Air Squadron was at Manston, it was inspected by a senior officer of air rank, and on this occasion, 13 July, the second batch of students were inspected by Air Vice-Marshal Vesey. He was accompanied by the Secretary of State for Air, Sir Samuel Hoare.

Number 605 Squadron, under the command of Squadron Leader Wright, visited Manston again in August for the unit's fourteen days' annual training, and it was inspected on 9 August my Air Vice-Marshal Francis Rowland Scarlett CB, DSO. The exercises, carried out in conjunction with No. 9 Squadron, took place on 13-16 August. No. 1 Air Defence Group, commanded by Air

Commodore Eugene Louis Gerrard CMG, DSO, opened up an Operations Room near the old War Flight site to help facilitate proceedings during the exercises.

There were a number of changes in key positions at about this time, and Squadron Leader E. N. E. Waldon was posted in as the Senior Accounts Officer. He replaced Squadron Leader Prall, who was attached to the Armoured Car Crew for training before being posted overseas. The Revd R. H. Horton took over the position of Chaplain at Manston to replace the Revd R. C. H. Warner DSO, who was also being posted overseas, to Egypt.

Rather unusually, Manston seems to have been inspected more regularly than might have been expected for an RAF station. On 14 September, the station was inspected again, by the AOC No. 23 Group, Air Commodore Bertie Clephane Hawley Drew CMG, CBE, who arrived by air. Just a few weeks later, on 6 November, he inspected Manston again. Then, on 20 November, Manston was inspected by the AOC Inland Area, Air Vice-Marshal Longcroft, who had only recently come out of retirement and off the Half-Pay List he had been on since 1923.

Number 2 Squadron (AC) was detached to Fridaywood Camp near Colchester where it spent three weeks during September. The camp was held from 1 September until the 22nd for co-operation work with the 4th Division of Eastern Command.

In October 1928, there was another series of lectures delivered to officers on air force law, this time by Flight Lieutenant G. Sims-Marshal who was from the Office of the Judge Advocate General. The first two lectures concerned the preparation of a case to take to trial, the first lecture being attended by thirty-two officers and the second by thirty-eight. The third and fourth lectures concerned the conduct and record of a trial by Court Martial and were attended by twenty-six and twenty-five officers respectively. Why such attention was given to officers being aware of air force law and regulations is not known, but most of those attending would have been from the administrative departments rather than air crew and technical trades.

On 8 November, the AOC Wessex Bombing Area, Air Vice-Marshal Steel arrived at Manston to inspect No. 9 Squadron. The fifty-one-year-old officer was another veteran who had served in the Royal Navy and trained at the Britannia Royal Naval College in Dartmouth. He had served on HMS *Conqueror* at the Battle of Jutland and had commanded the Royal Naval Station at Eastchurch in 1917, and No. 58 Wing which was based there. In 1920, he had been removed from the Navy List and awarded a permanent commission in the RAF.

In the same month, on the 29th, Wing Commander William Victor Strugnell took over command of No. 9 Squadron from Wing Commander Dursion, who was posted to the Staff College at Quetta in India, where No. 7 School of

Technical Training was based. Rather unusually, Strugnell had risen through the ranks, having joined the Royal Engineers as a boy and served as a sapper before rising to the rank of Sergeant and re-mustering to the RFC in 1915. During the same year he had become one of the rare breed of officers who were commissioned in the field for acts of bravery and valour. In June 1916, he was awarded the Military Cross and the following year was awarded a Bar to add to it. By the end of the First World War, Strugnell had been credited with destroying five enemy aeroplanes and a kite balloon and consequently had become an ace pilot.

At some point in early 1929, someone, possibly the Station Adjutant, decided to write up the RAF Manston Record Book in longhand rather than type it up as was the normal practice. The standard of writing is quite poor and, after being photocopied several times, a number of pages for 1929 and 1930 are barely readable. A few pages continued to be typed up, but because of the scribble in the other handwritten records, it seems that the details of some entries have been lost.

It was not a very good start to 1929 at Manston. The continuous bad weather had a serious effect on the running of the station. Severe weather conditions caused the collapse of the whole water supply and sanitary system so that standpipes had to be erected and field sanitary arrangements set up. Further subsidence also occurred in the area of the flagstaff on the central parade ground. It was noted in the records that the subsidence was similar to what had occurred in 1924, and the problem was to plague the station for many years.

An Officers' Promotion Board for category 'B' and 'C' examinations was held at Manston on 25-28 February, and Wing Commander Strugnell was appointed as President of the Board of Examinations to supervise the thirty officers that sat them. This was a busy time at Manston and, on 12 March, the station was visited by a sub-committee of the Air Ministry Establishment Committee. Members of the sub-committee remained at Manston for two days, and their main purpose was to consider the establishment for the station's HQ.

A number of projects were carried out by the Works Services in March that had been accounted for in the financial year 1928/29. They included a Coyton range, machine-gun stop and a radio transmitter ground station for the use of No. 2 Squadron. This is the first mention of radio transmitters being used at Manston, and although R/T was still in its infancy, there were rapid developments during the 1920s and 1930s. There was also a pump house erected, and an increase in the number of fuel filling points made available.

RAF Manston achieved a number of sporting successes in early 1929. The station's football team won the Deal and Walmer League's Victoria Hospital Junior Cup. The team had originally played in the Folkestone and District

League, their last match in that league being recorded in January 1928. At some point in 1928, there must have been a change of leagues and, in March 1929, it was noted in the records that RAF Manston were leaders of the Canterbury and District League.

Boxing was another popular sport at the station, and the Lightweight Sir Chas Wakefield Championship competition was won by Aircraftman A. C. Varley, who also won the RAF Lightweight Championship. Leading Aircraftman Buchanan won the RAF's Welterweight Championship, and Leading Aircraftman Dean the RAF Heavyweight Championship. The Inland Area Tournament was won by Flight Sergeant G. Salt.

In May 1929, the infamous Group Captain Richard Charles Montagu Pink arrived at RAF Manston to take over Command from Group Captain Hebden, who was being put on the Half-Pay List. Having served at RAF Manston since 1925, Hebden was the officer who, up to that time, had held the post of Commanding Officer for the longest period. Initially Group Captain Pink was appointed as the Commandant of the School of Technical Training, but within two months he had taken over command of the Station's HQ. It is claimed that Pink was the only Air Force officer to have had a 'war' named after him. Having commanded No. 1 Wing from November 1923, he was then given command of No. 2 Wing. In India his exploits became legendary and, based at Waziristan, Pink had taken part with his units in operations against dissident tribesmen. Their uprising was put down by his tactics of aerial bombing, and such was the success of the campaign that it became known as 'Pink's War'.

Having passed through the Britannia Royal Naval College as a Midshipman in 1908, Pink had served on HMS *Bulwark* before moving on to submarines as an acting 2nd Lieutenant. In 1913, he had been injured in an incident involving a submarine when his eyesight was affected and was subsequently placed on the Half-Pay List for seven months. In 1915, he trained to be an airship pilot and two years later had risen through the ranks to Commander, becoming second in command at Longside Airship Station and later the Commanding Officer of Pembroke Airship Station. By 1917, he had risen to the rank of Squadron Commander in the RNAS, before being appointed to the position of Director of Flying Operations and later as Airship Adviser to the Chief of Staff. Pink had been awarded a permanent commission as a Lieutenant-Colonel in 1919, and transferred from the Staff Branch to the Flying Branch of the RAF. After his exploits in India, he was posted to the Home Establishment in 1926 and promoted to Group Captain, before taking up a post at the HQ of the Air Defence of Great Britain.

Pink had his own aeroplane based at Manston during his time at the station, a very small single-engine type known as the 'Flying Flea'. It was powered by a 17 hp 500 cc motorcycle engine and had originally been designed and built by Frenchman Henri Mignet. Appropriately enough, it was painted pink.

In June 1929, the first detachment of a number of territorial units arrived at Manston for annual training. Among them were the five officers and 120 men of the 1st Corps of Signals under the command of Major C. Lewis MC, and also No. 507 (Tyne) Searchlight Company under the command of Lieutenant-Colonel Firmin OBE.

An incident not directly connected to RAF Manston, but one that would have undoubtedly involved the station, occurred when a Handley Page W.10 twin-engine passenger aircraft, G-EBMT, crashed into the sea off Dungeness on 17 June. The crew, consisting of the pilot and a mechanic, were in an exposed open cockpit. The aircraft was carrying eleven passengers on the route from Croydon to Le Bourget in Paris. From Paris it was then scheduled to fly on to Zurich in Switzerland.

After departing Croydon at 10.30 a.m., and approximately fifteen miles off the English coast, the pilot, Captain R. J. Bailli, broadcast a Mayday message saying that an engine had failed and the aircraft was losing height but he had turned back and was hoping to reach Lympne. Unfortunately the aircraft was unable to maintain level flight on a single engine and it dived into the sea approximately ten miles off the coast. There were only six survivors, who owed their lives to the crew of a trawler, the *Gaby*, which was on the scene immediately after the crash and helped to rescue them. The survivors included the crew and four passengers who had been seated at the rear of the aircraft. Wreckage was later towed ashore by the *Gaby* close to Dungeness lighthouse, and the subsequent investigation found that the accident had been caused by a broken connecting rod in the starboard engine.

A brief report on the accident appeared in *Flight* magazine three days after the incident, stating that the aircraft had turned over when it hit the water, trapping those passengers sitting at the front. It pointed out that Imperial Airways had flown 3.8 million miles since 1925 without losing a single passenger, but what it failed to say was that G-EBMT was the airline's third aircraft to be lost since October 1926. In the two previous accidents, only by the grace of God had there been no loss of life.

The Oxford University Air Squadron arrived at Manston again on 30 June 1929, still under the command of Wing Commander Garrod. By that time, the university authorities had recognised the unit as a permanent institution, equal in status to the Officer Training Corps. The 1929 annual summer camp caught the imagination of the public because the press had been invited, and some of its activities were also recorded for posterity on film by Pathe News. The brief video clip that can still be seen on the internet (www.britishpathe. com/video/undergraduate-airmen/query/01511600) shows a very mixed bunch of student pilots standing around by a number of Avro 504s while they were being briefed by a wing commander, presumably Garrod. Some of the students were dressed in flying clothing, while others were casually dressed in shirt, tie and sleeveless jumpers, with one particular character, wearing glasses and looking quite bemused! The news clip then shows seven aircraft taking off and flying across the airfield in loose formation. They are then seen flying across Pegwell Bay and Ramsgate Harbour where the video finishes as they bank to port and return to land at the airfield.

The press was so enthralled with the sight of the University Air Squadron's Avro 504s flying over Canterbury Cathedral that one paper described the scene as 'an instrument of modern war circling the tomb of the great chivalric warrior'. For the summer camp the Practice Flight was equipped with eight Lynx Avros, two Bristol Fighters (service type) and a single Bristol Fighter fitted with dual controls that had a slotted wing. Altogether, the Oxford University Air Squadron completed 1,105 flying hours without any serious incident.

As might be expected, most members of the unit were among the university's social and sporting elite. Among the squadron's personnel were two rugby Blues, two rowing Blues, and two boxing Blues. During the summer camp at Manston, three members of the squadron decided to make the RAF their career and subsequently passed their initial training with distinction. Not everyone in Oxford was so enthusiastic about flying, however, and it was feared in some sections of the city that if Oxford became a major flying centre, it would attract the attention of foreign powers and might be bombed.

On 1 July 1929, Establishment Order IA/914 came into being, which effectively separated HQ of RAF Manston from the School of Technical Training (Men). It seems that the School had grown to such an extent that it was justified in being made a separate unit in its own right, and although the station remained under the control of Group Captain Pink, Squadron Leader Measures was appointed as the Commanding Officer of the School of Technical Training. Before the war, Measures had been employed by a number of engineering companies before joining the staff of the Royal Aircraft Factory. Having joined in 1912, he was one of the first members of the RFC, and at that time was still in the ranks. He was still only a Sergeant Major when he was awarded Royal Aero Club Certificate No. 520, June 1913. His expertise was soon recognised, and from 1917 to 1929 he commanded the Eastern and Western Repair Depots.

Flight Lieutenant Charles Philip Oldfield Bartlett DSC was appointed as the Adjutant, and Squadron Leader C. E. W. Foster as the Administrative Officer. Bartlett had been awarded the DSC while serving in the RNAS as a Sub-Lieutenant on the occasion of a bombing raid on Houttave aerodrome on 25 July 1917.

On the last day of July 1929, RAF Manston was visited by a party of four officers from the Japanese Army Air Force, who were led by Captain Horra. During his visit to the School of Technical Training he was accompanied by three staff officers, and this was one of several visits by members of the

Japanese forces, the previous one having been in October 1927.

The Essex AA Searchlight Group, Royal Engineers Territorial Force, arrived at Manston in July, along with the Surrey AA Group for their annual training, and August was to be another busy month at RAF Manston. On the 11th, Air Marshal Edward Leonard Ellington visited the station to inspect the training being carried out by the regular, auxiliary and territorial units. Ellington had only recently returned from five years' service overseas when he had been appointed as the AOC Air Defence of Great Britain. The 26th Searchlight Battalion (Royal Engineers Territorial Force), under the command of Lieutenant-Colonel M. G. Bland OBE, and the 26th and 27th Searchlight (Anti-Aircraft) Signal Companies were among a number of units that arrived at Manston for annual training.

The Kent and Middlesex Searchlight Companies, under the command of Lieutenant-Colonel A. F. G. Rushton, also took part in the annual exercise, with the 27th Searchlight Battalion under the command of Lieutenant-Colonel C. H. S. Evans. RAF participation in the exercises was provided by No. 605 Squadron, which arrived at Manston again under the command of Squadron Leader Wright. The auxiliary unit was still based at Castle Bromwich and equipped with the ancient DH.9. A single Flight of No. 1 Squadron, normally based at Tangmere, was attached to Manston for co-operation with No. 605 Squadron and was equipped with the Armstrong Whitworth Siskin.

On 21 August, RAF Manston was inspected by the Chief of the Air Staff, Sir Hugh Trenchard. The purpose of this particular visit is not known, but Manston's location relatively close to London seems to have made it a regular meeting place for senior officers.

By that time a number of small businesses in the local area were partly dependent upon trade from airmen serving at RAF Manston. One of them was Kings, a shop on Meridian Walk, Ramsgate, which advertised in *Flight International* such items as RAF officers' uniforms in either wool or barathea. It also sold slacks in either material, made to measure for 32s 6d a pair, as well as many other items of service clothing, and it is a typical example of how local tradesmen were reliant upon RAF Manston for their living.

A Station Welfare Clinic was opened in September and was aimed particularly at looking after the health and welfare of those airmen who were married. The clinic was officially opened by the Chaplain in Chief of the RAF, the Revd R. V. Hanson OBE.

RAF Manston achieved more sporting success at the end of October, when the station won the RAF's Water Polo Championship held at Halton. Manston's opponents were from RAF Digby in Lincolnshire, and Manston won by two goals to one. The fact that Manston had its own indoor heated swimming pool helped to raise interest in water-based sports like water polo, and the team did not have to rely on facilities outside of the base.

There were, however, a number of things done at this time to encourage the local population to mix more freely with the personnel at RAF Manston in an attempt to do what was described in the records as 'installing air mindedness' among the younger generation. One such policy that was actively pursued concerned encouraging the pupils of local schools to visit the station in order to find out what went on there and what Air Force life was really like. The first children to take part in such visits were those from St Lawrence School in Ramsgate, who visited the station on 10 October. Other schools that participated in the scheme included Thanet Court, Westgate, which visited on 15 October; Surrey House, Margate, on the 24th; Birchington House on the 28th; and Warden House, Deal, on the 29th.

By this time, there was another airfield active in the area just a short distance up the road from RAF Manston, from where Alan Cobham and several other aviators are said to have flown. The airstrip at Nethercourt Farm has largely been forgotten, but at the end of the 1920s and into the 1930s it aroused a lot of interest among those who wished to be taken up on pleasure flights. It was later to become an important airfield operating scheduled flight to London. Its exact location is open to debate, but was somewhere between Manston Road and Canterbury Road East, where a housing estate was later built.

On 26 November, RAF Manston was inspected again, by Air Vice-Marshal Borton, who had taken over as the AOC Inland Area from Air Vice-Marshal Longcroft on 1 November. Borton was another of the 'Old Guard' who had joined the Militia of the Black Watch in 1904 and transferred to the Regular Army in 1906. He had learned to fly while on leave in late 1911, and was awarded Royal Aero Club Certificate No. 170 on 9 January 1912. He took up the appointment as the AOC Inland after having served as the Director of Personal Services for several years, and it was to be his last office before retiring from the RAF.

In December, Flight Lieutenant G. G. Walker MC arrived at Manston to take up the duties of Station Adjutant from Flight Lieutenant Bartlett. Bartlett was not going very far – he was transferred to the School of Technical Training where he took up the post of Adjutant. Squadron Leader Measures continued to command the School of Technical Training that had recently separated from its parent station. E. J. Cuckney was the School's Squadron Leader Engineering, and under him were Flight Lieutenants P. H. Owyer MBE and G. J. Southern. The two junior officers at the school were Flying Officers C. H. V. Hayman and A. B. Gliddon DSM. Flying Officer W. E. Symonds was appointed as the Officer Commanding the Station Practice Flight in December. However, there were soon to be changes made to that unit, and within a matter of weeks he was posted to the Depot at Uxbridge.

CHAPTER 14

The Glorious Thirties

On the first day of 1930, the Air Ministry Costing Committee paid a visit to RAF Manston and stayed until 21 January. There is no mention in the records of what section or unit was being scrutinised, but no doubt everything was examined in detail as these were still harsh economic times. Whether it had to do with the strength of RAF personnel at Manston is not known, but there is a brief mention of civilian labourers being employed as aircraft hands.

The Air Estimates for the RAF in 1930 were £18,177, significantly lower than the £21,471 proposed for 1920. The authorised manpower for the RAF in 1930 was 19,078, not very different from that of 1920, which had been 19,760 airmen.

Also on the first day of 1930, RAF Manston had another foreign visitor in the form of Major Gheorghiu from the Rumanian Air Force who was attached to No. 2 Squadron. Many people may not be aware that Rumania had such a force, but it was actually one of the oldest, having been established in 1913. During the First World War, Rumania had relied upon Britain and France for support, and they supplied it with 322 aircraft. Rumania was, however, in the process of building its own aircraft and the IAR.80 stressed-skin fighter was to equal those single-engine fighters that flew in the Second World War.

The AOC No. 23 Group, Air Commodore Philip Bennet Joubert de la Ferté KCB, CMG, DSO, visited Manston on 31 January. He had taken over the Group in December 1929, and was another member of the 'Old Guard' who had been commissioned as a 2nd Lieutenant in the Royal Field Artillery in July 1907. In 1912, he had fulfilled his ambition of learning to fly, being awarded Royal Aero Club Certificate No. 280, and was subsequently transferred to the RFC in March 1913.

Having been awarded a permanent commission as a Lieutenant-Colonel (Wing Commander) in August 1919, de la Ferté had served in a number of purely administrative posts such as those he had held in the Department of Intelligence and as Director of Personnel. He had been appointed as the AOC

No. 23 Group in September 1926, but at the time of his visit to Manston in early 1930, his tenure in that post was coming to an end.

Another Officers' Promotion Board was held in February in respect of category 'B', 'C', 'D' and 'E' examinations for those officers who were serving in units in and around the area of RAF Manston. It was held under the Presidency of Wing Commander Strugnell, the Commanding Officer of No. 9 Squadron who had previously overseen the Board.

The watch office (later called the control tower) was moved from the area of the former War Flight to land adjacent to the Station Practice Flight. It is interesting to note that some twelve years after the War Flight had been disbanded, its base on the eastern side of the airfield was still referred to by its old title. After the move, the Station Practice Flight was given a different role and renamed the Permanent Reception Flight, with its aircraft being clearly marked for identification purposes when guiding visiting aeroplanes into RAF Manston.

Building work in the Officers' Mess was approaching completion in February after the fire that had caused significant damage to the Annexe in September 1925. Work did not begin on the Annexe, which was the worst affected part of the building, until October 1929, and the rebuild and alterations to other parts of the building were finally completed on the 28th.

A total of fifty-three airmen passed out from the School of Technical Training in February, including forty-two drivers (petrol) and nine riggers, the latter being the backbone of the RAF who serviced and built the airframes of aeroplanes. During this time and in a period when most aeroplanes were built of wood, those who had experience as carpenters or joiners were ideal candidates to be trained as riggers. It might have been a sign of the times, but by comparison only a single blacksmith and a single coppersmith and metal worker passed out then. Among a small number of postings in and out of Manston at this time was Flying Officer Hayman, who was posted out of the School of Technical Training to No. 1 Stores Depot at RAF Kidbrooke.

The Station Commander, Group Captain Pink, began a period of liaison with members of the local Observer Corps in March, many of them having been involved in the recent air defence exercises. Pink made personal visits to all the local units and, as a gesture from the RAF, all members of the Observer Corps were made honorary members of the respective messes at RAF Manston. In the same month, the station was visited again by a sub-committee of the Estimates Committee to discuss minor adjustments to the establishment.

In March and April, two more courses passed out from the School of Technical Training with a total of sixty pupils completing their training in March. That figure was made up of eight blacksmiths – no mention of coppersmiths – and fifty-two drivers (petrol), and during April another thirty-three passed out, with nine coppersmiths – no mention of blacksmiths – and twenty-four drivers (petrol). There were so many drivers (petrol) under training that another department, established as No. 3 Section, had to be opened to cope with the influx. The original figure for the official establishment had been for 350 drivers (petrol) to be trained, but by the end of April that figure had risen to 622 and the School was forced to expand.

Flying Officer Symonds, formerly of the Station Practice Flight, was promoted to the rank of Flight Lieutenant. He was then posted to Worthy Down, where he was to take up flying duties.

On 26 April, at 7.30 p.m., the giant German airship *Graf Zeppelin* was spotted by an eagle-eyed observer at Manston, flying towards the coast of Belgium. The passenger airship, D-LZ 127, which had first flown on 18 September 1928, was on the last leg of a round-the-world flight, returning from the USA where its captain, Dr Hugo Eckener, had met the American President Herbert Hoover. The Operational Record Book notes that it was flying at a height of just 1,500 feet, but there is no mention of who spotted the airship or whether it was seen from the ground or from the air.

There were a number of movements in and out of Manston at this time, and also a number of visitors. Flight Lieutenant Staffen arrived to take over the post as Station Armament Officer from Flight Lieutenant Drumar, who was posted to Upper Heyford. Major Beeston-Bell of the Royal Corps of Signals visited the station to discuss arrangements for accommodation for the signals and AA units that were to undergo their annual training at Manston during the summer months.

On 1 May, No. 9 Squadron took part in an exercise at an armament practice camp being held at RAF Catfoss, near Hornsea in East Yorkshire. The following year, Catfoss was officially designated as the No. 1 Armament Training School.

May was a busy month for the station and, among other things, its swimming baths were thrown open to the children and families of airmen who were based at Manston. As with the earlier promotion of 'air mindedness' among the younger generation, this was another attempt to encourage a certain type of interest among them, but this time it was swimming. However, it does seem strange that the swimming baths were not generally open to the families of airmen in the first place.

On the 25th of the month, a detachment from RAF Manston was sent to Deal to attend a memorial service for the late Field Marshal John Denton Pinkstone French, the 1st Earl of Ypres, who had died five years earlier on 25 May 1925 in Deal Castle. Having served in the Royal Navy from 1866 until 1870, Lord Ypres, who was also known as Viscount French, had transferred to the Army and served with distinction in the Boer War, commanding a Cavalry Division. After the Boer War he had been made Commander-in-Chief of the 1st Army Corps and the Aldershot Command, and he rose rapidly through the ranks, being made a full General in February 1907, and a Field Marshal in June 1913. During the First World War he had been involved in numerous campaigns, including those at Aubers Ridge, Loos, and Ypres. After the war, in May 1918, he was made Lord Lieutenant of Ireland, but he was a controversial figure and was later replaced by Lord Edmund Talbot, a Catholic, who was seen as being more sympathetic to the Irish cause.

French retired from the British Army in May 1921, and after becoming the President of the Ypres League, a veterans' society for those senior officers who had served in the Ypres Salient, he was given the Earldom of Ypres in June 1922. After his retirement, French had planned to live in Ireland and had bought several properties there, but because he had made many enemies in the country, it was thought that he would be a target for Sinn Féin. In 1923, he had been persuaded to take up the honorary post of Captain of Deal Castle, where he lived until dying of bladder cancer in May 1925.

Although French was in the Army, he had always been 'air minded' and closely involved with the Air Force, being particularly concerned about the air defence of London. He had campaigned for greater priority to be given to air defence, and when Brigadier Ashmore was appointed to command the air defence of London, it was French to whom he had to report, and he was greatly respected among officers in the RAF.

Wing Commander Archibald Corbett-Wilson was posted to the School of Technical Training at RAF Manston with effect from 31 May, taking over as Commandant from Group Captain Pink. It is notable that he did not hold a Royal Aero Club Certificate, but he did have both a Royal Aeronaut's Certificate (No. 37) and an Airship Pilot's Certificate (No. 22). Both had been awarded when he was serving as a Lieutenant in the Royal Field Artillery on 29 November 1913. The concept of airships was becoming popular again, and the R101 was about to begin a series of test flights at Cardington as Corbett-Wilson took up his post at Manston.

Squadron Leader Measures was put on the Retired List at the beginning of June. Having served in the RFC and risen through the ranks, he was effectively promoted and allowed to keep the rank of Wing Commander. Measures had been in aviation all his life and did not give it up after retirement. He was employed by Imperial Airways as the senior technical assistant to the Chief Engineer. He used his experience of Africa to the company's advantage, and was involved in putting in place the organisation for the inauguration of the Empire Route from Karachi to Singapore.

RAF Manston was called upon to provide a guard of honour on a couple of occasions, including at a commemoration service in Canterbury Cathedral on 2 June, although there is no mention of the purpose of the ceremony. The most likely reason was to commemorate Randall Davidson, the former Archbishop of Canterbury, who had died at the end of May. He held the post from 1903 to

1928, and had been awarded the title of Baron Davidson of Lambeth.

The other event was the Royal Tournament at Olympia in London, and it is stated in the Operational Record Book that on the 11th, 'At very short notice the station trained and provided a guard of honour at the opening of the Royal Tournament by HRH the Duke of York.' This is rather confusing because the tournament ran from 29 May to 14 June, and according to a clip from Pathe News it was opened by Prince George, the Duke of Kent. He is seen inspecting a guard of honour made up of very smart airmen, who may have been from Manston or the Depot at Uxbridge, which normally provided airmen for such occasions. Regardless of such details, RAF Manston did play a role in the 1930 Royal Tournament.

On 14 June, Group Captain Pink and his wife held a garden party that was thrown open to members of the aviation fraternity, and 800 guests accepted invitations. Among them were the Director of Civil Aviation, Air Vice-Marshal Sir William Sefton Brancker KCB, AFC, and the Principal ADC to the King, Air Vice-Marshal Sir Edward Ellington. There were many other well-known names from the world of aviation, including Sir Alan Cobham who had trained at Manston during the Great War. Miss Winifred Spooner, a pioneering female aviator who had become only the sixteenth woman to gain her flying licence, had also been invited. She had been awarded licence No. 8137 by the London Aeroplane Club in 1927 and was a great sporting competitor, having finished fifth in the 1929 King's Cup Race.

A number of guests arrived in their own private aeroplanes and approximately thirty aircraft were parked on the airfield in special enclosures so that they could be easily viewed by the guests. Although there was a flypast by a formation of Vickers Victoria transport aircraft of No. 70 Squadron, the weather closed in during the afternoon and low cloud and rain prevented any further displays or other visiting aircraft being able to land. Despite that, the party helped to create further good relations between the RAF and the wider civil aviation community.

On 18 June, No. 9 Squadron lost another pilot when Flying Officer John Cecil Lauga Claxton was killed as a result of a flying accident at Farnborough. Why he was at Farnborough is not known, but he was flying a Bristol F2.B Fighter rather than one of the squadron's Virginias and the aircraft belonged to the School of Photography. Little is known about this officer, other than that he had joined the RAF on a short service commission (on probation) in July 1928 and was then posted to the Depot at Uxbridge. His promotion to the rank of Flying Officer had been announced in *The London Gazette* on 29 December 1929.

There were a number of liaison visits between RAF Manston and the Royal Navy. Officers and ratings of the 33,020-ton Queen Elizabeth Class battleship HMS *Malaya* arrived at the station in July in an attempt to encourage better co-operation between the two services. There was a series of impromptu meetings between officers from both services to discuss the current organisation and how it could be improved.

Launched at Wallsend in March 1915 and commissioned in February 1916, HMS *Malaya*, with its eight 15-inch guns, was a formidable opponent. It had been lucky to survive, however, as during the Battle of Jutland in May 1916 it had been hit no fewer than eight times. After a refit in 1929, the battleship had returned from the Mediterranean and was about to be deployed as part of the Atlantic Fleet. There is no mention of where HMS *Malaya* was berthed, but presumably it must have been either tied up at Dover or at anchor in the English Channel.

RAF Manston sent a team to Bisley in June to take part in the National Rifle Club Championship, which had been held there since moving from Wimbledon in 1890. The competition ran from the 2nd to the 6th. There is no mention of how well the team did, but shooting was a popular sporting activity at Manston, which had its own rifle club. Many years later, when I was posted to the station, it still sent a team to compete.

A number of Army units were attached to Manston again during the summer of 1930, including No. 1 Company from the Royal Corps of Signals, which was attached from the 5th to the 21st. The 307th Searchlight Battalion arrived soon afterwards and was attached from the 21st until 7 July.

The Oxford University Air Squadron arrived at Manston on 21 July for its two-week summer camp, and its activities were widely reported by *Flight* magazine, which had been invited to attend and observe the squadron training on Thursday 24 July. By then, the first two courses of fifty students (twenty-five per course) had passed through and carried out a considerable amount of flying and landing practice. However, by the time that *Flight* arrived, the third course were experiencing very bad weather, the 24th being a gloomy day with intermittent rain.

The squadron was equipped with a number of Bristol Fighters that had a wide dark blue band painted across the full length of the wings from the roundel on the starboard wing to the roundel on the port. Despite the bad weather, *Flight* reported that the ability of the Oxford University Air Squadron pilots was quite remarkable.

A number of students had to withdraw, including one who left because he was taking important examinations and another who was found to have problems with his sight that made landing very difficult. New members had been taken from the waiting list at short notice and, despite the fact that some of them had never flown before, all achieved the necessary 3 hours' solo flying. In addition to this requirement, in order to qualify for the Certificate of Proficiency instituted in 1928, students also had to pass written examinations in airmanship, engines, rigging, and air pilotage. By 1930, forty-eight members of the squadron had gained the certificate, but stricter rules had been put in place demanding that a student must resign if he did not qualify in the period allowed.

Twenty-two members of the squadron were already members of the RAF Reserve and flying with auxiliary units, and *Flight* reported that the Air Ministry had opened a channel to facilitate getting other members of the squadron into the air very quickly if an emergency arose. Among those who took part in the University Air Squadron summer camp in 1930 was Flight Lieutenant Francis John Williamson Mellersh, who had flown with No. 9 Squadron (RNAS) in the Great War and been credited with five enemy aircraft destroyed. On what later became No. 209 Squadron he was in Roy Brown's Flight and witnessed him shooting down the 'Red Baron'. Having been awarded a permanent commission as a flight lieutenant in 1926, he had joined the squadron in May 1929 as an instructor.

In the article in *Flight* magazine, the CO of the University Air Squadron, Wing Commander Garrod, had nothing but praise for RAF Manston. He said it was the most satisfactory station to train pilots because of its climate, health, and opportunities for recreation. There were tennis courts, swimming baths and plenty of places to sea bathe. During the summer camp the squadron's students were not billeted in tents but in the Officers' Mess. The 1930 camp was the last one for Garrod, and within a few months he was to be posted to Iraq where he worked in the Air Staff in Operations. Sadly it was also to be the squadron's last summer camp at Manston. The following year the tie was broken and the camp was held at Eastchurch.

The Royal Engineers attached to Manston held their Annual Sports Gala on 11 July, and the month was generally taken up with several other sporting events. On the 17th, the annual Swimming Gala was held in the station's swimming baths, and the following week the RAF's Swimming Championships took place. They were not held on the station at Manston, however, but in the swimming baths in Cliftonville at the top end of Margate. It is not known why the RAF chose a civilian establishment rather than Manston, but the most probable explanation is that the station's swimming facilities were not big enough or up to the standard expected for such an occasion.

Air Marshal Ellington paid a brief visit to Manston on 27 July to make final arrangements for the forthcoming Air Defence of Great Britain exercises. He had previously held the post of AOC Middle East, AOC India and AOC Iraq, whence he had only recently returned, and had been one of the first few hundred pilots to learn to fly, having been awarded Royal Aero Club Certificate No. 305 in October 1912. What stands out on Ellington's service record is that despite the fact that he had learned to fly, he had no experience of commanding a squadron or being a Flight Commander. Virtually all the posts he held were in administrative or staff roles, and he had little or no experience of serving on an active flying unit. That, however, did little to prevent his promotion, and following his appointment as the AOC Air Defence of Great Britain on 1 February, on the 27th he was appointed as the Principal Air Officer and ADC to HM King George V.

A number of other units arrived at Manston in July for annual training, and No. 603 Squadron was another that was attached to Manston station from the 12th to the 27th. An auxiliary unit based at Turnhouse near Edinburgh, it was equipped with the ancient DH.9A and a small number of Avro 504s that it used for training.

Wing Commander Corbett-Wilson took command of HQ RAF Manston at the end of July, although his term of office was neither one of the longest nor one of the most exciting. It is not known why Group Captain Pink handed over command of the station, because he was still active at Manston in one role or another for a further year. Within a short while, however, he was found to be suffering from cancer, and it may well have been that he gave up his office because of the illness.

The Air Defence of Great Britain exercises were held from 11-15 August, and may not have produced the result that the Air Marshal was hoping for. RAF Manston was acting as a 'Blueland' station and No. 12 Squadron, the only unit to be equipped with the Fairey Fox, provided part of its bombing force, along with the Boulton Paul Sidestrands of No. 101 Squadron. Two squadrons of Armstrong Whitworth Siskins provided the 'Blueland' fighter force. The attacking 'Redland' force was being acted out by a number of units, including the Gloster Gamecocks of No. 23 Squadron, Hawker Harts of No. 33 Squadron, and the Fairey IIIFs of No. 207 Squadron.

The 'Blueland Colony Force', under the command of Air Vice-Marshal Steel, had its HQ at RAF Andover, while the 'Redland Colony Force' was under the command of Air Vice-Marshal Dowding and was based at RAF Cranwell. Although the exercise officially began on Monday the 11th, hostilities were not declared until 11 a.m. on Tuesday the 12th. It was noted in Manston's Operational Record Book that it was one of a number of stations that were heavily bombed on that day by 'Redland' forces. Five 'Blueland' aircraft were destroyed on the ground at Manston and another eight damaged (umpires decision only). On the 13th, there was heavy fighting in the area of Sheerness and Manston, and during one engagement lasting no more than 5 minutes, a force of nine bombers from 'Blueland' was engaged by an equal number of 'Redland' fighters, resulting in two bombers and one fighter being shot down. A 'ceasefire' was called at 3.30 a.m. on Friday 15 August when a 'proposal' by the League of Nations was accepted by both sides and the exercise was terminated.

Number 605 Squadron had become a regular visitor to Manston and was also attached to the station over the period of the exercise from 1-16 August. Still based at Castle Bromwich, it was by then equipped with the Westland

Wapiti. Surrey Group HQ Searchlight Companies were at Manston from the 2nd to the 17th, and the AA Signal Artillery Company from the 16th to the 31st, making RAF Manston a very busy and crowded station.

Squadron Leader Sydney Edward Toomer took over command of No. 2 Squadron from Squadron Leader Probyn on 29 September, while the latter was posted to No. 25 Squadron at Hawkinge. Toomer's background was particularly interesting, having begun his military career as a gunner with the Highland Regiment (Mountain). He had joined the RFC as an observer in February 1917, and by December he was classed as a pilot under training.

The former Commanding Officer of No. 9 Squadron, Wing Commander Guilfoyle, gave a lecture about the organisation of the RAF Reserve in early October. The Reserve had been established in 1924 with the setting up of auxiliary squadrons, and he had been appointed to the post of Superintendent in January 1929. It was a position that he held until March 1933, when he attended a Senior Officers' War Course. He eventually rose to the rank of Air Commodore and retired from the service when he was fifty-two years old, in 1942.

CHAPTER 15

A Nation in Mourning

Sunday 5 October 1930 was a day that was to be remembered by the whole nation, because on that day the giant airship R101 crashed near Beauvais in France. RAF Manston had particular connections with the chain of circumstances that led up to the disaster, especially in the aftermath of events when it provided a guard of honour on the return to England of the bodies of those who were killed.

As previously mentioned, Wing Commander Corbett-Wilson was an airship pilot himself and understood many of the difficulties that airship crews faced. It is also believed that he was a friend of the Captain of the R101, Flight Lieutenant Herbert Carmichael Irwin, and also of the Director of Civil Aviation, Air Vice-Marshal Sir William Sefton Brancker. Brancker had learned to fly while he had been serving in India, and was awarded Royal Aero Club Certificate No. 525 in June 1913. Irwin, an Irishman and a great sportsman, was a former RNAS pilot who had served in the Great War, and in 1924 had commanded another airship, the R33.

Just a week before the R101 set off from Cardington, Brancker had visited RAF Manston to meet Corbett-Wilson. There was mounting pressure to get Lord Thomson, the Secretary of State for Air, to India and back in time for an important conference, and there is little doubt that Brancker was seeking advice from an old friend. Brancker was flown down to Manston by Winifred Spooner, who, like him, had attended Group Captain Pink's garden party in June. From 16-18 August 1930, she had been flying in the International Tourist Plane Contest in her de Havilland Gipsy Moth, finishing seventh overall. It is believed that she flew Brancker to Manston in the very same aircraft in which she had competed.

At Manston, Brancker had tea with Corbett-Wilson as well as a number of other senior officers, all of whom expressed their concern about the R101's scheduled flight to Karachi in India. It was later claimed that Corbett-Wilson thought that Brancker was not very happy about the serviceability of the airship, that things had been pushed too much, and that the R101 still had gas leaks.

There is no doubt that apart from the gas leaks, there were still a number of problems with the R101, and because of the failure of an oil cooler in one of the airship's five Beardmore diesel engines, full endurance and speed trials had not been carried out. The final test flight, which was supposed to have lasted 24 hours, ended after 16 hours and 50 minutes, but despite that, on 2 October, the R101 was granted its Certificate of Airworthiness, which was handed over to and examined by Flight Lieutenant Irwin just a short while before it set off.

At 6.36 p.m. on the 4th, the R101, with its registration G-FAAW painted on its side in large black letters and trailing the RAF pennant, left the mooring tower at Cardington and set off on the long voyage to Egypt for its first refuelling stop. The most senior passengers on board included Lord Thomson, Sir William Sefton Brancker, and Major Bishop from the Aeronautical Investigation Department.

After flying a circuit over Bedford to gain height, the R101 set course for London, where it arrived at 8.20, sending out a message, 'All is well'. At 9.47, it sent another message saying that it had crossed the English coast in the vicinity of Hastings. The nearest airship station at that point was the Class 'C' station at Capel-le-Ferne, 2 miles from Folkestone. Progress was slow and it took 2 hours to cross the Channel, with the R101 reaching the French coast at 11.36 near Pointe de Saint-Quentin.

At 2 a.m. the watch was changed and 2nd Officer Maurice Staff took over command. A new course was set to take the airship over Orly, but a miscalculation in the speed and direction of the wind caused an error that was not immediately recognised. When it was discovered, the officer on watch changed course again to take the airship over Beauvais Ridge, a notorious feature that was well known for its downdraughts, updrafts and dangerous variations with the wind. While in the vicinity of the ridge, the airship went into a dive and lost approximately 450 feet, but it slowly recovered before going into a second dive when there was a call from the helm to reduce speed.

A combination of factors caused the airship to hit the ground at a speed of approximately 13 mph and at an angle of 15-20 degrees. Although the impact was minimal, the R101 immediately caught fire and forty-six of the fifty-four people on board were killed soon after it crashed, while another two died later in hospital of their injuries. The probable cause of the fire was that one of the engines made contact with the fabric, igniting the escaping gas from the airship. Oil from the engines soaked into the ground, and the fire was so ferocious that it was still burning the next day when the first party of officials from England arrived to examine the scene.

The bodies of those killed in the crash were conveyed by French gun carriages to Boulogne before being returned to England on the Tuesday evening on the 1,096-ton 'R' Class destroyer HMS *Tempest* (not to be confused with a submarine of the same name). Fifty airmen from Manston lined the quayside, and a photograph taken by the *Dover Express* shows a line of them with heads bowed and rifles reversed, while a party of bearers are walking towards the camera carrying a coffin. When they were landed at Dover, the same guard of honour accompanied the cortège on a special train that transported the coffins to London. It is not known who gave the orders for such action, although given the connection between the station's Commanding Officer and those on board, that would not have been necessary.

On Friday 10 October, a memorial service was held in the church at RAF Manston for those who had died in the R101 airship, and the Mayors of all the local towns in Thanet were invited to attend. A memorial card with the order of service was presented to all those who attended, which had the following written on it: 'Royal Air Force Manston Friday 10 October 1930. In Memory of those who died in the Disaster to H.M. Airship R101 on October 5th 1930.'

On the same day that the service was held at RAF Manston, the bodies of the forty-eight victims were taken to Westminster Hall in London where they lay in state. They were later taken in solemn procession to Euston station, from where they were transported to Bedford. There, gun carriages were waiting to take the bodies to St Mary's Church in Cardington where they were buried together in sight of the Royal Airship Works from which they had departed.

It is difficult to recall events after the tragedy of the R101, but, as today, trivial affairs of day-to-day life had to go on, and at RAF Manston things were no different. The General Post Office opened a sub-branch at Manston on 16 October, which would have been a popular move and saved personnel from having to visit the post office in Manston village. Miss J. Cumbernauld, the RAF's Matron in Chief, visited Manston, being concerned about the health and welfare of its personnel in light of various illnesses that had recently occurred.

One thing she could not prevent was airmen being killed in air crashes, and on 4 November, RAF Manston suffered its own tragedy when a Vickers Virginia of No. 9 Squadron, J5761, crashed near the airfield close to the old War Flight site, killing the two crew members, Flying Officer Frederick Robert Walter Goad and Sergeant Roberts. Little is known about either airman, other than that the former had only recently been promoted to the rank of Flying Officer on 7 October. Goad was buried locally in Minster Cemetery. It is understood that Roberts, who came from New Ferry in Cheshire, was buried in his home town. The Virginia involved in the incident, which had entered service with No. 7 Squadron in May 1925, and with No. 9 Squadron in March 1930, was repaired the following year and flew again in May 1932. It was eventually written off after another accident, when it had landed heavily in a cross wind at Worthy Down.

Flight Lieutenant G. T. H. Pack, an officer with considerable experience of aircraft design, was posted to Manston in November for engineering duties. In 1925, while stationed at Cranwell, he had been involved with and responsible for the wooden construction of the CLA.3 light monoplane built for the Cranwell Light Aeroplane Club to compete in the Royal Aero Club's race meeting at Lympne. The previous year, Cranwell's CLA.2 had claimed the reliability prize at Lympne, and those involved had won £300.

The incident on 4 November with Virginia J5761 was the last one involving No. 9 Squadron aircraft and personnel at Manston. On 26 November, the squadron moved out of Manston and was posted to RAF Boscombe Down, sadly bringing to an end six and a half years of service at the station. Another bomber squadron would arrive at Manston within a few months, but it was only an auxiliary squadron of the RAF Reserve and it lacked the security that came of the station housing a permanent unit.

Air Commodore Peregrine Forbes Morant Fellowes, who had been appointed to the post of AOC No. 23 Group in September and taken over from Air Commodore de la Ferté, visited Manston on 9 December. Another of the Australian contingent, he had gained his Royal Aero Club Certificate, No. 1697, in September 1915, and in 1917 had commanded No. 2 Squadron (RNAS). Fellowes had had several lucky escapes. In May 1918, while making an attack on the lock gates at Zeebrugge, he crash landed in the North Sea and was taken prisoner by the Germans. After the war, he was mentioned in despatches for 'valuable service while in captivity'. In August 1919, he was on board a Felixstowe Fury flying boat that crashed on take-off, and one of the crew was drowned. Before being appointed as the AOC No. 23 Group he had served as the ADC to the King, but was approaching the end of his service, and within a short while he was to be put on the Retired List.

The number of pupils who had passed out of the School of Technical Training during 1930 was 636. The total comprised 83 carpenters, 12 blacksmiths, 27 coppersmiths, 481 drivers (petrol), 10 fabric workers, 13 fitters (AE), and 10 riggers (aero). In addition, there were a number of naval ratings, members of the Fleet Air Arm formed in April 1924, who had attended courses for fabric workers. Over the course of 1930, there had been 1,089 personnel posted into RAF Manston, and 1,002 posted out, making a total of 2,091 movements excluding attachments.

At the end of the year, Wing Commander Corbett-Wilson, who was about to hand over command of RAF Manston, assumed command of the School of Technical Training. He was also about to be promoted to the rank of Group Captain, and within a short while he was to be posted to Boscombe Down.

Flight Lieutenant Bartlett remained as the Adjutant at the School of Technical Training, with Squadron Leader Cuckney acting as the Chief Technical Officer. Other officers at the school were Flight Lieutenants Pack, Owyer, and Strang

Graham MC, and Flying Officers Gliddon and Caddy. Flight Lieutenant Fenn remained on the strength as a civilian assistant.

By late 1930, many of those officers who had served at Manston when it had been a Royal Naval Air Station had risen up through the ranks. Former Squadron Commander Robert Ross Peel, who in 1915 had commanded the RNAS station at Westgate and had been influential in moving the landing ground to Manston, was an Air Commodore and the Deputy Director of Manning. Squadron Commander John Tremayne Babington of the Handley Page Flight, who had carried out the very first flight of the HP O/100 bomber, had been promoted to the rank of Air Commodore and appointed to the post of Air Representative at the League of Nations. He had served in Iraq and India, and commanded RNAS Gosport, and like many other officers who had served at Manston, had achieved high office.

Despite the short-sighted attempts of the bureaucrats in the Treasury to close RAF Manston down, the station had gone from strength to strength. Over the thirteen and a half years it had been established, RAF Manston had become not only a permanent station but one of the most important. Over the next decade it would prove to be one of the most strategically placed airfields in the country, and it was destined to play a vital role in the next major conflict.